POETRY NOW

ABSENT FRIENDS

Edited by Andrew Head

First published in Great Britain in 1996 by
POETRY NOW
1-2 Wainman Road, Woodston,
Peterborough, PE2 7BU

All Rights Reserved

Copyright Contributors 1996

HB ISBN 1 85731 634 7
SB ISBN 1 85731 639 8

FOREWORD

Although we are a nation of poetry writers we are accused of not reading poetry and not buying poetry books: after many years of listening to the incessant gripes of poetry publishers, I can only assume that the books they publish, in general, are books that most people do not want to read.

Poetry should not be obscure, introverted, and as cryptic as a crossword puzzle: it is the poet's duty to reach out and embrace the world.

The world owes the poet nothing and we should not be expected to dig and delve into a rambling discourse searching for some inner meaning.

The reason we write poetry (and almost all of us do) is because we want to communicate: an ideal; an idea; or a specific feeling. Poetry is as essential in communication, as a letter; a radio; a telephone, and the main criteria for selecting the poems in this anthology is very simple: they communicate.

Faced with hundreds of poems and a limited amount of space, the task of choosing the final poems was difficult and as editor one tries to be as detached as possible (quite often editors can become a barrier in the writer-reader exchange) acting as go between, making the connection, not censoring because of personal taste.

Everyone should have a special friend to pick you up when you are down. We all know that a true friend is one forever. So whether that person is always with us is not important, just that they are a friend. Everyone should be able to relate to this anthology, as we all have 'Absent Friends . . .'

The success of this collection, and all previous *Poetry Now* anthologies, relies on the fact that there are as many individual readers as there are writers.

CONTENTS

The Memory	Susan L Howarth	1
I Close My Eyes	Sarah Prescott	2
To Absent Friends	Edward Huntington	2
The Doorway	Jan Eve	3
My Mate Mick	Kath Bonney	4
Friendship	Edna Cass	4
Silent Friendship	Linda Fleming	5
Absent Friends	Lynsey Taylor	6
Just Good Friends	Michael Horton	6
Ruth	Marian J Lovelace-Knight	7
Canine Love	Tracy Butler	8
Friendship	Maisie Tompkins	9
Absent Friends	B Booth	10
To A Dear Friend	Amanda Jane Bruce	10
Golden Years	Margaret Couper	11
A Message Of Love	Christine Kemp	12
Loving Friendship	Maisie S Soall	12
Our Little Sooty	P Andrews	13
Prince	Nicola Brandon	14
Friends	A Baker	15
Three Weeks Ago	Philip Eley	15
Time	Naz Latif	16
Across The Sea	Beryl Jones	17
Adam	K Osgood	18
Untitled	Jay Palmer	18
Friends	Sarah Byrne	19
Sam	L Bolesworth	19
Happiness Ever After	Sarah Kind	20
Rob	R Jeffreys	20
Absent Friend	Margaret Anne Featherstone	21
Grandma	B Holland	22
'Til Then	Janet Muncer	22
Friendship	Angela Barrett Cordiner	23
Workmates	Barbara Vian	24
Friend In Memoriam	Beverley Gill	24
Sheila	Joan Butler	25
True Friends	Vicky Carlin	26

Emblem Of Friendship	Lisa Marie Stott	26
The Last One	M C Wood	27
Edges	Tony Mayle	28
I'm Gonna Be Someone's Friend	D J Rouchy	28
Council Pals Now Gone	Donald Jay	29
Jenny	S M Hunt	30
My Best Friend	Marjorie Whyte	30
Years Gone By	A P Lockey	31
Regrets	Jennifer Aston	32
Absent Friends	Tedward	32
Nature's Friend	Chas Dainty	33
My Friend	Teresa Wilson	34
Blue	Angela Hamer	35
Lasting Friendship	Marjorie H Smith	35
Goodnight Dear Friends	Violet M Corlett	36
Where Are You Now?	Doreen Bursnell	36
A Striking Old Man	Alasdair Aston	37
Old Friend	Ken Pendlebury	38
On The Loss Of A Mother	John Hampson	38
Untitled	Lisa N Charles	39
Now My Time Is Over . . .	Marylyn Pullum	40
For A Friend	Sheila Cook	41
Friendship	Elizabeth Petrie	42
Life Long Friends	Pamela Mitchell	42
The Golden Years	S Heaven	43
Friendship Now Distant	Susan Eason	44
Friendship	Wendy Colbert	45
More Than Just A Friend	Bonny Metin	46
For Ricky	Margaret Stevens	46
Helga	Jacqueline Gonzalez-Marina	47
My Spanish Friend	Shabnam Walji	48
For Glad	Patricia Samuels	49
Dear Dad	Richard Lowis	50
A Valediction	Valerie Skinner	50
We'll Make It	Stiggy Zeum	51
Mrs Eileen Davies	Melanie M Burgess	52

Friendships That Have Stood The Test Of Time	Catherine Stanton	52
Special Friends	A R Potter	53
A Distant Voice	Neil Blackshaw	53
Time, Sea Or Land	M Whitehead	54
Faraway Places	Mercedes Jordan	54
A Treasured Friendship	Kay Holmes	55
Absent Friends	Norman Letts	56
Saturday Thoughts	Audrey Roberts	56
Gone Forever	Hazel Webb	57
Friend	Steve Clarke	58
Silent Thoughts	Winifred Wardle	58
Friend	Trish Birtill	59
A Friend	Barbara Ward	59
Untitled	Linda Brabrook	60
For Joan Mary	Joan Margaret Howard	60
Friendship	R D Hiscoke	61
Thoughts Of You	E T Usher	62
Overseas	Francesca Holmes	62
Do Not Weep At My Grave	Mungo	63
So Many Goodbyes	Sally Quilford	64
Friends	Mandy Southern	65
Friends	Anne James	66
To Joan	P Brabin	67
To Maurean	Lillian Winstanley	68
True Friends	Katie Tench	68
The Roses Still Grow	Alissa Pemberton	69
The Tree - Friendship With Nature	Joseph G Dawson	70
A Special Bond	Dawn Downie	71
Benji My Best Friend	Richard Leach	71
Someone	Babs West	72
Golden Days	Marjorie Springham	72
Drifting Memories	Angela-Jane Norris	73
To Be A Friend	J Wells	73
Living On Memories	Desmond Hawthorne	74
Lost Friend	C J Wade	75
Friends	Catherine Spivey	75

Title	Author	Page
The Last Good-Bye	Jayne Watson	76
Friend	Helen Ireson	77
Pat	Julie Antcliff	77
To Ann	A C Wilkinson	78
The Lost Friendship	John G Pocklington	78
September Sunsets	Paul Beretta	79
Everyday Best	Rebecca Miller	80
My Goodbye Message	Jayanna Hughes	81
Absent Friends	Dennis R Rowe	81
Passionate Friends	I Barton	82
Then She Said . . .	Pluto Moran	82
Phone Friends	Michelle Liddle	83
Absent Friend	Sandra Vickers	84
The Gift Of A Friend	Paul Bailey	84
Comrade	Myk Jonson	85
Friendship	Alma Cooper	85
Best Of Friends - For Always	Victoria A Hicks	86
The Prize Of The Wise	T A Napper	86
Memories Of Friendship	Elizabeth Pocklington	87
Vow Of Friendship	Jimmy Metcalf	87
True Friendship	Donna Walton	88
Something Special	Julie Swan	88
The Mates I Left Behind	P Rockley	89
Absent Friends	F Merrett	90
Friends Forever	Harry Clarke	90
To Terry	Mandy Smith	91
Friends Across The Sea	M A Atkinson	92
Don't Cry Too Hard	Hazel Donnelly	92
My Two Best Friends	Valerie Warner	93
The Nightingale	Annie Atkins	94
Lady	R Mason	95
My Drinking Companion	Peter Key	95
Twilight	Jack Pragnell	96
Span Of Time	Dennis F Tye	97
What The Passage Of Time Can Do	Tina Whelan	98
Friendship Song	Linda Mussett	98
Ben	Simon Knights	99

Life	V Beck	100
A Friend	Jean Skates	101
The Meeting Place	Lily Jakubowski	102
Remember	Jacqueline M Arkell	103
To The Next Thirty Years	Anne Greatorex	104
Maye In The Killing Fields	Reuben Crowe	105
My Life Long Love	Julie Parkinson	106
A Need To Grow	Damian Green	107
My Paternal Friend	Shelley Brown	108
Hearts Apart	Duncan Callander	108
Forever Friends	Sharon Foot	109
Forever My Friend	Dian	110
To Choose A Friend	Elaine Gisbourne	111
When The Blackbirds Sing	Derek Atkinson	112
The Album	Linda Hunter	113
Gone But Not Forgotten	Shehla Aslam	114
Regrets	Marjorie Wagg	114
Absent Friend	Kathleen Gosling	115
Faithful Friend	Marian Freeman	116
Portrait	E W Griffiths	117
Angel In A Frame	Darrell Ryan	118
I Hear A Tiny Heartbeat	Karen E A Levick	119
Untitled	Mary Whorlow	120
Always	Fiona Pearce	121
A Friendship Everlasting	Dawn Oliver	122
Still (For Betsy)	Maroushka Monro	123
Friends!	Alanna Allen	124
Thinking Of You	Brian Magee	124
For Mary	Pamela Broster	125
Friends For All Of Time	Patricia Willis Taylor	126
The Photograph	Rosemary Lane	127
On Earth As It Is In Heaven (A Debate)	Kenneth Lane	128
Cry Tears	Derek Reeves	129
Proud To Call You Friend	B Luffman	130
A Shoulder To Cry On	Valerie Hall	131
Automatic	Natalie George	132
You And Me	Sheila G Farrow	132

A Thank You Poem To		
My Best Friends	Maureen Weitman	133
The Garden Gate	Hilda Mawer	134
A Dear Person	M Goodwin	134
Forever Friends	Angela Edwards	135
Absent Friends	Clarice Rothwell	136
My Dearest Mum	Jean Christie	136
Annette	D M Dudley	137
Ode To An Absent Friend	O J Adams	138
Friends Forever	Tara L Huddless	139
Always Friends	Philip M Smith	140
Do You Remember?	R J Curry	141
Vanessa	Laura Charleton	142
Reunion	Sylvia Hillman	142
Over Thirty Years	B M Bryan	143
Goodbye Aunt Rose	Wendy Fry	144
Friends	Derek Charles Fuller	145
For Midge	Doreen Britton	145
You And Me	Maggie Cardew	146
Pals	Ted Rolls	146
Still Friends	Connie Moseley	147
Comradeship	P Temperton	148
Friends	Joanne Aisthorpe	148
You And I	G D Wakefield	149
Friends Forever	Margaret Collins	150
Friendship	Helen Towner	150
Untitled	Anne-Marie Rose	151
Friendship	Peter Ley	152
A Memory Of A Friend	Luciene Azique	152
To An Absent Friend	Heather Horlock	153
Me And Pete	Anthony John	154
Patricia	John Hampson	155
Pot Of Gold	Hilda Naughton	156
Untitled	Bridget Ward	156
Distance And Discos	Samantha Bate	157
Friendship Blues	Terry Bobrowicz	158
Untitled	Carol A Maddison	158
A Friend	Pauline Jones	159

Friends And Lovers	Loraine Darcy	160
My Absent Friend	Laura Parkinson	160
Keeping In Touch	F Norris	161
To Friendship	Ann Williams	162
Lasting Friendship	M Weavers	163
My Old Ted	F M Rapley	164
Soul Mates	June Mills	164
My Old Acquaintance	Martin Ford	165
Threads Of Gold	Lesley Lyn	166
End Of An Era	D M Gibbons	167
Pen Friends	Jenny Major	167
Friendships Gain	Carolyn R Byrom	168
A Belated Friend	Chris Waltham	169
Celestial Abodes Of Absent Souls	Rhys Wyndam Warren	169
Forever Friends	Maureen Stewart-Condron	170
Remember Love	J Sanderson	170
Special Friends	Lindsey Robinson	171
Soul Mate	Eileen Bolan	172
Days	Zoe Young	172
Friend - Sister - Mother	Odette Timmons	173
To My Friend Miss Clark	Yvonne Harding	174
I Think Of You Often	Jayne Smith	174
Destiny	Vanessa Lloyd Williams	175
Poem One	Elizabeth E Wallbank	176
Friendship	Brenda Barker	177
Grace	Sheila Williams	178
Remember	Drew Michaels	178
Order Of Service	Wordsmith	179
Katy	J Humby	180
Soul Mates	Anne Goodale	181
Friends Abroad	Sally Newton	182
Friendship	Jenny Gill	183
Special Friends	Corinne Tuck	184
Together Forever	Kelly Hall	185
Big Pete - Last Orders Mate	John Arthur Gilman	185
Forty Years On	Gwen Hare	186
Friendship	Yvette Herbert	187

A Friend	Pim Foster	187
Lifelong Friendships	Beatrice May Roberts	188
Past Friend	R H Elliott	189
Four Years On	Michelle Taylor	190
A Long Day	D R Wareing	191
Sorrella	Gill Moreland	192
Across The Room	Rachel Cole	192
Friends	Barbara Shaw	193
True Friendship	Amanda-Marie Foster	193
Always There	Karen Bayly	194
Just A Friend	Jackie Drabble	194
My Best Friend	Jacqueline M Arkell	195
Distance No Object	Chrissy Smith	196
Odd Letters	Jackie Silverwood	197
Friends	Harriet J Kent	198
Bobby	S Curling	198
Grandson	Jack Segal	199
My Special Friend	Michelle Henderson	200
The Window	Janet Forrest	201
Friendship	May Harrison	201
Little Joe	Marguerite Auton	202
Ode To Diana	Jane Webster	203
Forever Friends	M Warne	204
Ted's Reward	D Barrett	204
Claire	Fiona J Saunders	205
A Friend Is Not Just For Christmas	John W Skepper	206
Old And New	Barbar Fenner	207
The River	R Faulder	208
Absent Friends	Emma Smyth	208
Friends	Paula New	209
Friends	L Thwaites	209
My Best Friend	Daisy May	210
Friendship	Anne Frances Wilson	210
Fond Friends	Joan Wallington	211
Recalled To Mind	K Hemmings	212
Rope Ladder	John P Green	213
Untitled	Mary O'Neill	214

Memories Of Our Friendship	Marjorie Coulthard	215
For Andrée-Anne	Nina-Ann Lewis	216
My Absent Friend	Vivienne Brocklehurst	217
Friends	Josie Jessop	218
Untitled	J C Darby	219
Girl Jen	Heather Lee-Hooker	220
Friendship	Dorothy Ventris	221
Derek	Mavis Boothroyd	222
A Friendly Match	Belinda Hastie	223
A Distant Friendship	Doris Paul-Clark	224
A Long Distance Friendship	Holly Foat	225
Poem To My Friend	Irene Hanson	226
Sixteen	Doreen Palmer	227
Friendship? Or Are There Really Angels?	Jon Tuffnell	228
Best Friend	Paul Thompson	229
Untitled	Olivia Hughes	229
Thrown Together	Valerie Duffy	230
Ode To An Unknown Friend	Carol Rivas	231
Night	Pauline Avril Denham	232
Absent Friend	Deanna Margaret Hassan	233
Mum	Jennifer Maureen Young	234
When The Light Went Out	A B Stearns	235
Is It Friendship Or Love?	Lena Frances	235
Long Time Now	Christopher G James	236
An Enigmatic Variation	Jill Wheatley	237
Caring Friends	Elaine Howard	238
Hands Across The Water	Peter De Beer	239
Wishing, Wanting, Longing	John S Lovesey	240
My Friend	Angela M Harris	241
Alone No More	Lannette Lusk	242
Untitled	Sue Millett	243
Remembering The Terrain	Bernard B Michael	244
Memories Of Bill	Frank Rimmington	245
My Friends From Across The Sea	Geoffrey Quint	246
All My Friends	M A Tubb	247
Friendship	Alice Englefield	248

A Lasting Friendship	M L Fletcher	249
Absent Friends	I E Covell	250
My Absent Friend	Valerie E Brown	251
Genuine Friend	C M Ellard	252
Pity The Living	Janet Greenwood	253
An Ode To The Stone Tents (And The Friends I Shared With)	Pauline Barker	254
Goodbye	H M Berry	254
Memories	M Caulfield	255
Absent Friends	Mairearad Wilson	255
The Never-Moulting Wing Of Friendship	Ivor Haythorne	256
Under The House	Gillian Wilde	257
My Faithful Friend	Trish Chandler	258
What Is A Friend?	J Hart	258

THE MEMORY

I watched you grow up through your teenage years,
And you know how often I shed my tears.
I'm not the mixed up girl you once knew,
I saw you often and our friendship grew.
Those nightmare years I've left behind,
You helped me through, and strengthened my mind.
My soldier, my hero, you were at that time,
Good and kind-hearted, would you end up being mine?
You held me close, I felt so secure,
Tender loving kisses, as I leaned on the door.
You had to leave, I knew this would come,
I had no one to turn to, nowhere to run.
The army . . . it took away my friend.
For weeks and months my heart wouldn't mend.
On your return thoughtful gifts you bought,
I was so mixed up, not ready to be caught.
Your eighteenth party was really good fun,
Just like in my garden, in the summer sun.
I enjoyed your company, we got on so well,
But of a future together, no one could tell.
As you were leaving my house one day,
You pushed the door closed, you had something to say.
Your arm on the door, looking straight in my eyes
I didn't know what was coming, it was such a surprise.
'When I'm twenty-one should we get engaged?'
But with thoughtless remarks I mentioned your age,
You left my house, you closed my door, my absent friend I had no more,
No phone call, no letter, you left my life, I wasn't ready to be your wife.
With sadness I imagine what could have been,
Your love and kisses, vivid memories and dreams.

Susan L Howarth

I CLOSE MY EYES

The laughter that danced through your eyes I can no longer see,
until I close my eyes.
Your face that was so kind and friendly I can no longer touch,
until I close my eyes.
The home-baked bread that I watched you make I can no longer smell,
until I close my eyes.
The heaviness of your tired feet that I can no longer hear,
until I close my eyes.

Your silvery hair that shone in the sun I can no longer see,
until I close my eyes.
The warm draught of must that was upon your clothes I can no longer smell,
until I close my eyes.
Your voice that was so clear and strong I can no longer hear,
until I close my eyes.
The friendship that you gave so freely I can no longer touch,
until I close my eyes.

I close my eyes one more time and I feel your presence in me,
You are in the world I see and in the sounds I hear,
You are in the smells I breathe that touch the very heart of me.
I need no longer close my eyes.

Sarah Prescott

TO ABSENT FRIENDS

I've travelled far in lorry and car,
In train and plane and boat.
I've marched through countries day and night,
Made friends of every sort.

Black and white, yellow and brown
They're all the same to me
We fought for years side by side
To make all people free.

Where are they now? I often ask
Grown older just like me
Like ships that pass in the night
Across the deep blue sea.

'Raise your glass to absent friends'
For a moment time stands still
Memories of bygone days
Some tears your eyes may fill.

Edward Huntington

THE DOORWAY

We stood on the wide stone doorstep
The porch arching over our heads
Our hands hovered over the bright brass bell,
'Press me for your answer,' it said.

It has been many years since we saw them,
These friends from so long ago,
Will they want to renew our acquaintance?
Our time has neglected them so.

Put into remembered compartments,
Though never completely away,
So many times have we meant to phone
Or go for 'that visit' some day.

Once close in thought and direction
Everything shared with one heart,
We were young and together we spoke of our dreams,
But the dearest of friends drift apart.

The door swung wide - inviting,
The faces, so dear, here at last,
Older of course, and arms open wide
To welcome two friends from the past.

Jan Eve

MY MATE MICK

I was 3 and you were 7
31 years later you went to Heaven.
From 18-22 you were my best friend,
Hazy, lazy summer days, we thought they'd never end.
Then to a far-off land, you went away to stay,
Oh, how I missed your smiling face and chats we had each day.
Fleeting visits, letters, telephone calls, as time swiftly passed us by,
Right up to the day you died - and I asked *why?*
I mourned you, grieved for you, couldn't let go,
Until someone said 'Let your tears flow
Although he's gone to pastures new,
He's still smiling, watching over you.'

Kath Bonney

FRIENDSHIP

Not given to us every day,
It takes some time to test and try
The strength of bonds that won't give way
In storm or strife - and this is why

A friend who knows the worst of us
And grins and bears each glaring fault
Might sometime glimpse the best of us
And come to think we're worth our salt.

And so continue in that role
Till decades pass, with all things shared:
By then, between us, just one soul
To pray the other might be spared,

For only death can separate
A love that grew between two friends
And either heart will beg of fate
To go together when life ends.

Edna Cass

SILENT FRIENDSHIP

We'd have great fun, my friend and I,
We'd play around all day.
We'd go together to the park
And laugh and run and play.

As years went by we'd still converse
And tell of all our sorrows.
My friend would listen patiently
To all my planned tomorrows.

Together we would face the world;
No worries left unheeded.
My friend was always there for me
When help was really needed.

We moved around this world of ours
To many foreign climes;
I needed help and sound advice
A million different times.

Our friendship deepened through the years;
Though many miles apart,
My friend was always there for me,
And had been from the start.

This faithful friend has older grown,
As surely have we all,
But true friends never notice age,
Don't mention it at all.

He's thread-bare now, this friend so true,
My much loved Teddy Bear,
But like the very best of friends,
I know he's always there.

Linda Fleming

ABSENT FRIENDS

Dream on, dream on,
And tell me of you,
In your dream I am,
I will show you the path through.

I am your spiritual friend,
I will show you the light,
I'll be with you till the end,
I will help you through the night.

In times of trouble,
I will always be there,
To help and to guide you,
So don't ever feel fear.

Lynsey Taylor

JUST GOOD FRIENDS

Our bodies sharing one soul, meet
in witness to Nature's masterpiece.
To kiss on cheek yet long for lips,
magic from our warm smiles drifts.
I weave my words for a woman, kind
who lights desires with fiery eyes.
Hear the music of our conversation,
no words adorned to hide their meaning.
Rip open our souls with every word
and savour speech without pretension.
Ensnared within our own wrought webs
those passions never dared unbound.
Restrain all thought of our true dreams
and forever remain the best of friends.

Michael Horton

RUTH

Friend of mine, long gone,
Yet what a feast you leave behind.
A feast of memories, of wisdom,
Which often springs unbidden into my head,
So unexpectedly.

Your body, misshapen, distorted, crumpled -
A lop-sided figure hobbling through the park,
Looking twice your age, each step an agony,
'Like walking on marbles constantly,' you said.

Angular hands, like claws,
Crooked, wracked with pain,
Tired, drawn, yet when you greeted me,
The beauty of the real you shone forth.

The beauty of your face,
Was beauty borne of pain -
Not that of cosmetic gloss,
The beauty of wisdom - home-grown,
And painfully gained by introspective thought.
Not of classroom learning,
No theoretical bilge of academia,
But honest homespun truth,
En-light-ening,
New visions of old familiar words
En-rich-ing, re-create-ing,
Awakening my mind,
Withdrawing from the inward eye
The veils put there to combat life and survive -
Tenderly.

Marian J Lovelace-Knight

CANINE LOVE

Geoff, you are in fact my best friend
Who I will love till the end.
Don't worry I'll always be there,
And for you I'll always care.
Someone to shout at when you're mad,
Someone to cry to when you're sad.
Someone who enjoys seeing you smile,
And with you will walk many a mile.
Through sun, wind and rain
No matter what pain,
With you each day
Sniffing the way.
Normally walking close by your side,
Rewarded by my stick of hide!
To show what I like, I wag my tail
My only dislike is going for a sail.
I eat lots and lots, and am known as a hog
But what do you expect, I'm only a dog!
I warn you when someone knocks at the door,
And run to greet them, on my legs all four.
I sometimes chase cats who are out the back,
But all in all, I'm glad you're in my pack.
As you're not really a bad old stick.
So to show my love - here's a big sloppy lick.
A friend helped to write this rhyme for thee,
With lots of love and woofs from little me!

Love Sheba.

Tracy Butler

FRIENDSHIP

Friendship is a lovely thing,
Many pleasant hours it brings.
I had a friend of long ago
But, to London she travelled and met her beau.
They sailed away to distant shores
And then I heard of her no more.
Through the years my thoughts did stray
Of this friend of far away.
I conjured up visions galore
And wished and wished, I could see her some more.
Imagine my surprise one day
When a letter from New Zealand came my way.
I opened it up, and what was I told?
This friend of mine had traced my abode.
She was coming to England to visit, it showed.
Our meeting was marvellous, and sublime
As we greeted each other after all this time.
We reminisced, and reminisced,
Then added our families to our list.
Time was spent reviewing old scenes
And lots of new ones to be seen.
We are older now, and our lives are changed
But we still have a twinkle remaining the same.
She has hobbies, and so do I.
Of these we chatted, she and I:
Back to New Zealand she now has gone,
But memories of her visit will last life long.

Maisie Tompkins

ABSENT FRIENDS

Whenever I've needed someone to confide my troubles to,
Or whenever I am miserable and feeling rather blue,
I just pick up the telephone or write a letter to my best friend.
My anxieties soon seem to fade away because on her I can depend.
although she's sometimes out of reach and can't always get in touch,
I know she's thinking of me and that always helps so much.
She's not always full of sympathy about some of the things I tell,
But listening to my troubles is a thing that she does well.
Years of happiness and heartache in the past we both have shared
But the best thing about our friendship is knowing that she's cared,
In all my life one of the best things that I have ever had,
Is this friendship from my best friend which will forever make me glad.

B Booth

TO A DEAR FRIEND

How I depended upon you
How safe I thought I was
I was wrong -
Look what you have done.

I really needed to talk to you
I really needed some comfort
I was wrong -
To have thought I could rely upon you.

Only wanting an arm around me
Only wanting you to be there
I was wrong -
To understand that you could help.

Believing I could count on you
Believing you were my friend
I was wrong -
I do not want you any more.

Amanda Jane Bruce

GOLDEN YEARS

Imagine two girls,
Delightful; like pearls;
Shy, blushing English roses.
Mutual interests grow -
Fifty years ago;
Friendship gently encloses.

Picture young women,
Hard-working; living
Surrounded by sham and fake.
Meeting for a meal
To chat and reveal
Friends give; they tend not to take.

One 'pearl' stayed near home;
(And her telephone);
T'other the Tropics did scan.
So letters took charge
Friendship to enlarge;
Invisible-flame to fan.

Imagine these two,
Middle-age they knew;
In-touch by phone and visits.
Now sagging in parts,
But deep in their hearts
Friends to unbounded limits.

Both 'oldies' agree
'Gold' friendship's not free;
Consistently there is love.
Twinned humour and care,
Bless the 'pain-rid' pair
With 'unseen' gifts from above.

Margaret Couper

A MESSAGE OF LOVE

A message of love at this special time of year
To old friends and new I wish you good cheer
May good health and fortune follow you through
To a future full of happiness for each one of you
May peace prevail on earth day by day
Remembering old friends who have passed away
We will never forget as the years go by
For the memories we have will never die
So rejoice and be happy the future looks bright
As we sing in the new year and celebrate the night
So sing my friends old and new for the message of love I send to you.

Christine Kemp

LOVING FRIENDSHIP

How I miss his tender smile,
His loving care, mine for a while,
A word or two would put things right,
Banish worries out of sight,

Suddenly my whole life changed,
All alone it feels so strange,
No loving arms to hold me tight,
No soothing words to put things right,

But deep inside the love we shared,
Helps to ease daily cares,
He was the best friend that I had,
Losing him made me so sad,

But all the years we spent together,
Gave me true love that lasts forever,
I trust when it's time to depart,
I will meet once again,
My friend and sweet-heart.

Maisie S Soall

OUR LITTLE SOOTY

We had a little bunny and Sooty was her name,
And now she's joined our toots and Scruff,
Things just won't be the same.

We had our Soots from six weeks old
And loved her very much,
Now when we open up the door,
There's just a sad old hutch.

Our bunny to the wire would come
When we'd go to the gate,
She'd put her little paws up
And greet us like a mate.

We miss her little face and big brown eyes,
They'd look up at us with love,
But now she's gone to play at last,
With her bunny friends above.

She'll always be within our hearts,
And with Toots as well she's joined,
They'd make us laugh, our Soots and Toots,
When Soot's hutch our Toots purloined.

But we never will forget you
And hope you miss us too,
And if you'd care to visit us
A fuss we'll make of you.

P Andrews

PRINCE

I opened the gate and you were gone,
Out into the world all alone.
You seem quite happy to be there,
Because you've not come home.
I only wish I knew where you were,
Because I miss you and wish you'd return,
To sit next to me and listen and learn.
I can remember when you first came,
Into my life with nothing but a name.
I gave you a home, kennel and food,
A friend for life is for what you became good.
You would sit each day and watch as we ate,
With your soft brown eyes and your big wet nose,
Begging until it was just too late,
Sent to your basket -well that's how it goes.

Then one day I returned from school,
The gate was open, you were nowhere to be seen,
And nobody knew where you'd been.
I looked around and called your name,
But you'd run away - no one was to blame.

You lived with us for four or more years,
And when you left there were many tears.
All memories of you are still in me,
Your different expressions I can still see.
Although mayn't have shown it all of the time,
I was proud when asked in you were mine.
With your glossy black coat and your big paddy paws,
You broke all the rules and made your own laws.
But fate intervened and you had to go,
I just hope you're OK 'cos I loved you so . . .

Nicola Brandon

FRIENDS

My destiny was all arranged
When I was in the womb
I didn't know my future
Would be full of doom and gloom
I've struggled endless hours
Holding back my tears
Feeling rather lonesome
My mind full of fears
My friends gather round me
To try and cheer me up
I'm very pleased to have them
When I am in a rut.

A Baker

THREE WEEKS AGO

Did I forget to mention
I left three weeks ago last Sunday
When you were laughing at my dancing
And wishing we were younger
I shook hands with your father
My only other friend
Your mother played a symphony
With a whistle and a tin
Don't expect greatness from your children
They were asking me for guidance
I told them not to grieve the living
They're only friends in waiting
Till you can stop forgiving as
A reason to keep hating
Never expect anyone to give you a second chance
Friends are only strangers
Who asked you for a dance.

Philip Eley

TIME
(Dedicated to the loving memory of my niece)

One minute, one hour, one day,
One month, one year,
And now so many years.
Who could have thought, it would have gone so fast,
Gone so quick,
Gone without so much of a blink?
It seems like yesterday,
You were with us, and we were with you,
And now we're apart,
And yet it still feels untrue,
I keep on thinking, you'll be appearing,
That you'll be the next one through the door,
I keep seeing shadows,
I think it's you,
But when I turn to see,
It's as always, anyone but you.

I carry on with life,
But you are with me, for always,
They say time will heal and make a difference,
And make me forget how much you meant,
I know that's untrue, because I'm still feeling blue,
Could that be because I'm still without you?
It's always the same,
The same from everyone, they all say,
Carry on with your life,
Time will heal, and make me forget,
All the pain of losing you,
But now I know that's untrue,
Because I'm still feeling blue.
Could that be because I'm still without you?

Naz Latif

ACROSS THE SEA

A friendship strengthened by the years,
As we shared our hopes and fears.
Young student teachers when we met
Retired now, we won't forget
Our friendship's formed so close a tie
Only ending when we die.

She came from Belfast across the sea
Her home is now so dear to me
We talked of differences of faith
She said 'There is no other place
Where the grass is oh so green
And tiny shamrocks can be seen'.'

I took some English grass with me
As I sailed across the sea
We laughed and chattered on and on
Long after the sun's last rays had gone
Our paths of life led different ways
Strong as iron our friendship stayed.

Sometimes we do not meet all year
Yet still we know each other's near.
I'm feeling sad or need a chat
What to do? I just ring Pat.
Thank you for sharing all these years
My smiles, my dreams as well as tears.

Beryl Jones

ADAM

Words somehow escape me,
No matter how I try,
My page lies barren, empty -
Just like a starless sky.
Believing in forever,
Is something I can't do,
Or couldn't - not until,
The day that I met you.
You have taught me reason,
When I saw no rhyme,
You have taught me friendship,
Can cross the plains of time.
No matter where I am,
I'm always by your side,
My love for you is endless,
Just like the rolling tide.
What we have is precious,
And I know that I'll endeavour,
To be here for you always,
We are - 'Friends Forever.'

K Osgood

UNTITLED

I know you'll always be here,
When they've all let me down.
Loyalty's your middle name,
You're the only one who could make me laugh,
In all the years I can recall,
I can trust you even if I trust nobody else,
Sharing my pain, understanding me,
If I fall apart, I know you'll piece me together again,
All I ever had was you,
Who'd of thought my only friend lives in a mirror?

Jay Palmer

FRIENDS

You're someone who'll just listen
Day or night you'll always be there
Not having to se each other often
Just knowing you'll always care.
Memories, secrets and joy
Together we've shared over the years
Always being prepared to comfort
When time brings forth the tears.
Throughout my life no one better
Can I always trust and depend
A place which cannot be filled
By any other, than my friend.

Sarah Byrne

SAM

There was no wrong and no reason in our childhood games,
    but the memories of those days will always remain
We played in the sunshine, the rain and the snow,
    with our imaginations there were always places to go
There were rainbows to follow, treasures to find,
    we'd play for hours, leaving reality behind
I'll never forget you, the time spent with you my friend,
    and now that you're gone memories help my heart to mend
Time had no meaning, all day we would play,
    now years have passed, but it's as clear as yesterday
But now you have left me and our childhood's a thing of the past,
    I promise you I won't forget you, my memories will last
You only have one friend who with secrets you share,
    there's only one friend, for whom you'll always care.

    Goodnight

L Bolesworth

HAPPINESS EVER AFTER

We shared our schooling years
And all those tears,
You said you had to go,
But where - I just didn't know.
I stood at the school gates
With all our giggly mates,
Our hands were held high
As we waved you goodbye,
You said you'd write
And I held those words so tight,
So I jumped with joy -
Like a kid with a new toy
On one winter's day
Because your letter came my way.
Five years later
Our friendship's even greater,
Your pigtails are no longer there
As your head is covered in golden hair.
Time has gone by so fast:
This time I know our friendship will last.

Sarah Kind (14)

ROB

When I got up, I thought of you
When I went to bed, I thought of you
I wished that I could dream of you
But I never did!

I tell my friends but they just shout
'We don't know what you're on about!'
If only I had asked you out
But I never did!

You saw me as a married lady
And you probably thought I was totally crazy
I wanted to tell you how unhappy he'd made me
But I never did!

Sometimes it was easier to ignore you completely
But I want you to know that I think of you sweetly
I want to scream across the miles
'Come back, dear Rob, I'll pay for your smiles.'

But I never do!

R Jeffreys

ABSENT FRIEND

Old friend that ages well with time,
Remember when you and I,
Ran through the rambling hills,
Saw the sun shine glints of gold,
Over the heather and through the ferns and trees.
We talked of life, present and past.
A friend that shall always be a part of my life.
Never the night shall fall or the dawn break,
Without a thought or two of my old friend.
His love, his friendship, his kindness
Shall reap in everything I do.
His needs are so simple and sincere,
All he had to do was smile,
The luck and laughter forever there.
Now the glints of gold are his pathway to heaven,
As he walks to the hills of eternity.
Then as the sun sets and dusk does fall,
So, will I remember him for old time's sake,
My best friend called me 'Sunbeam'
I simply called him 'Dad'.

Margaret Anne Featherstone

GRANDMA

When 'Auld acquaintance' is sung at Christmas and New Year's day
I shed a tear, think of my mother-in-law
Who was born on Christmas day and married on Christmas day.
She was eighty years old when she died
She was my mother-in-law and my best friend.
I think of all the love and caring
She gave to her family she was very very kind.

I think of all the happy times we had and
The troubled times we shared.
I could talk to her she would listen,
She seemed to be the only one who cared.

I still miss her as the years go rolling by.
My memories of her never fade and
I sit and heave a sigh.
She loved all her grandchildren very much
And I can still hear her voice saying,
'Now don't you touch.'
We have to say goodbye sometime to
The ones we love and know
But memories and friendship can never
Fade away, no matter how many years ago.

B Holland

'TIL THEN

I don't know what I'll do,
When we meet again.
What words I will choose,
When we greet again.
And when all our news is told,
Should we dare to take hold
Of the past again?
I don't know.

Janet Muncer

FRIENDSHIP

We met when we were in our teens
And went to school together
We've known each other for 30 years
And still we meet each other

There was a time when you moved away
And I thought I'd lost a friend
But we kept in touch by letter
Saying we'd be mates to the very end

The times did change and we did wed
Although they did not last
They were our boyfriends from long ago
And now they are our past.

We've laughed and cried
Upon each other's shoulder
And we can still do the same
Even though we're older.

We have had holidays together
In the Summer sun
And sat and reflected on things
That have now been and gone

We always come back to the thought
That each of us are there
To help us through the bad times
A somewhat caring pair

I'm thankful for our friendship
So all my love I send
To one very special person
A true and caring friend.

Angela Barrett Cordiner

WORKMATES

It's thirty years - yes, thirty years
since Gill and I first met:
how many thousand laughs and tears
have there been? - I'll bet
we've shared more in our lives
than many people ever get:
at first it was easy, the daily tasks
we discussed as we sat and ate
our lunch in a city coffee house
putting the world to rights; and yet
it wasn't very long before we found
our thoughts had become a duet.

Our lives have gone their separate ways
and now we're thousands of miles apart;
but it's still as though we're at adjoining desks;
for we each hold the other close, deep in our heart.
My sleep time's her waking, and vice versa.
Summer and winter, different weather we chart.
We dare not phone as we'd chat till we dropped
but we exchange tapes, and her children's art
adorns my home, as our photos do hers.
Our friendship's so strong it makes my eyes smart
and I know it's a thing I will always treasure:
two separated people, distance will never part.

Barbara Vian

FRIEND IN MEMORIAM

Borne in my mind you are to me now, my friend,
My spirit rises up to meet you and dance.

You may have died, expired this earth, my friend,
But loving memory of you pierces my soul - a red hot lance!

My dreams run like streams and rivers flowing out (like tears),
Through valley, canyon and sea.

It is through dreams, my friend, when I witness your face
I know that you come back to me.

Beverley Gill

SHEILA

When we were young happy and gay
Thoughts of age were far away
Dancing and singing our lives were a whirl
Oh what became of those joyful girls.

Fate caused you to travel afar
Our door of friendship was always ajar
Notes, letter, postcards came
But nothing would ever be the same.

Quickly as our families grew
Thoughts often returned of you
You made the journey home by air
We met again and life was fair.

Now once again we are apart
Only by distance not by heart
Our friendship has been true
For forty years plus two.

We know not what the future holds
Our friendship will not grow cold
Only death will break the final strand
To be reunited in God's hand.

Joan Butler

TRUE FRIENDS

True friends like you are hard to find
You're always there at the back of my mind
We've been best friends since our days at school
You were always there when I played the fool
Yet now we live in different places
We have new lives and see different faces
But one thing I know that is definitely true
I'll never have a friend as good as you.

Vicky Carlin

EMBLEM OF FRIENDSHIP

Whatever I have on my mind
I know in you I can confide
you're such a caring, special friend
on your trust, I can depend.

Best friends we are, yet different,
in so many different ways,
religion, creed and colour,
and your night times are my days.
Yet this is not a problem,
we find the time to share
by airmail or by telephone
just to show we really care.

Our happiness, our sadness
to each other we will turn,
no matter what the problem,
we listen with concern.
We will see each other again this year
and the feeling this will bring,
such tears of joy and happiness
for our friendship is everything.

Lisa Marie Stott

THE LAST ONE

There was Alice and Doris,
And sweet Mary Sue,
Annie and Edy
And Marguerite too.

From being sixteen
We had been very close,
A friendship that lasted
Much longer than most.

We'd seen good times and bad,
But always we're there,
In need and in trouble,
Our problems we'd share.

Throughout marriage, divorce,
Struggle and strife,
Somehow we kept in touch
In each others' life.

The years have flown by,
Our numbers have dwindled.
But three of the motley crew,
Have survived the rigours of this life,
Soon, probably only two.

This night, I retire with a heavy heart
Past memories flooding my mind.
A silent prayer slips through my lips
For friends fallen by the wayside.

A quiet moment for souls long gone
Then a whisper escapes my lips,
Please, when my time doth come
Don't let me, be the last one.

M C Wood

EDGES

Honeyed corners, that were sweet and stood out from the restlessness.
Nothing to do so we glided around
where the edges met the road.
We sharpened our minds on the corners,
often looking up at the gilded window frames.
Kieran said that he would work there someday
and would tell how the outside looked from within.
We laughed at him then,
knowing he had a rolling a seven on a dice chance.
No chance.
But we would have encouraged him if we had seen his short life then.

I got here and found it was nothing special.
The carpets never smelled the way I imagined,
threadbare in places where people could never have walked.
The furniture had the subtle flash of the vandal's taint,
from away, ordinary and unremarkable.
Up close, even more so but with time's scratch repeated.
Kieran would have hated it.
But,
if I see him again, I don't think I'll tell him.
I would never spoil his picture or
file the edges away from the honeyed corners.

Tony Mayle

I'M GONNA BE SOMEONE'S FRIEND

Today's the day to start again
I'm no-one's wife, I'm no-one's friend
I have no job, I have no home
I'm all alone, cold streets I roam.

I'm gonna make a new start
I'm gonna be someone's friend
I'm gonna see the world
This is now, that was then

I had a job, I had a life
I was a friend, I was a wife
Those days have gone, I'm all alone
I need a friend, cold streets I roam

I'm gonna have a warm home
I'm gonna have a good life
I'm gonna make a new start
I'm gonna be someone's wife

Today's the day to start again
I'm no-one's wife, I'm no-one's friend.

D J Rouchy

COUNCIL PALS NOW GONE

In days gone by, when I was young, the rural life I led.
On the Council I did work with Bill and George and Fred.
There was Bill the binman, what a lad, was lifting bins with me
of ash and muck and other things you would not like to see.
Donald the drainer, with rods in hand to unblock your drains,
he was your lad. Now to Donald the smell was like a fine scent to him
but would you do his job, unblock your bog?
There was tar boiler Bill and paver Peter with buckets and bars there
was no-one neater.
And Fred the flagger they worked all day in sun and rain,
it was not like play.
Road sweeper Bob with brush in hand in the town centre he did stand
and sweep till day was done.
And don't forget the lads on nights, salting the roads to your delight.
The Council worker had small reward.
But in truth it is to tell, but for the lads who do this work
your town would smell like hell,
So take some time to think of this the next time you want to complain.

Donald Jay

JENNY

Dear Jenny our beloved friend.
Gave us love until the end.
Through all the laughter and the tears.
She stayed so loyal through all her years.
We romped together in the park.
Oh how I miss her happy bark.
Although I miss her dearly.
The memories I can't hide.
She's still so very close to us.
Sitting by our side.
We remember all the joy we've ever had.
Losing our most loving friend.
Has made us very sad.

S M Hunt

MY BEST FRIEND

In August I lost my best friend,
She had loved me from the day I was born,
Until the day she died.
Her love was unending and unquestioning,
The kind of sacrificial love that surpasses all.

She was so much a part of my life,
That her leaving me has left a void,
Where sadness and happiness mingle,
Memories of happy times, so precious, bring a smile,
Sadness, because there can be no more, a tear.

I shall never forget the last time we were together,
The look in her eyes said 'You mean the world to me';
But now she has gone, never to be replaced,
My best friend has left me,
Goodbye Mum.

Marjorie Whyte

YEARS GONE BY

It's been a long time now,
the years have passed us by.
I remember the day you went away
it seems just like yesterday,
you left me all alone and blue.
The smile on your face
and your warm embrace,
will stand the test of time.
The tears in your eyes
tell me you want to stay,
but you still went away,
breaking my heart in two.
Oh my darling how I miss you,
the more I think about it,
I know your were meant for me.
If you will return to me
we can carry on where we left off,
and it will seem like yesterday,
but that's not soon enough.
Please come home my darling,
absence makes the heart grow stronger.
That's how the saying goes,
I'm waiting for your return,
my darling,
and that's not soon enough.
Goodbye for now.

Cheerio!

A P Lockey

REGRETS

'You don't know what you've got till it's gone,'
Is a phrase that is often used,
Be it a job, a car, or a friend,
They're all very sad to lose.

If it's a job that you have lost,
Don't sit and fret and stew,
Read the papers, get out and about,
Then one day you'll start anew.

When it's a car it's surprising to see.
How some people can feel so depressed,
But it's only an object, that can be replaced,
No reason to be so obsessed.

But when it's a friend who has deserted or died,
You've reason to feel sad and blue,
A friend is a person who helps you get by,
Who laughs and enjoys life with you.

Hold close to your friends and try to be kind,
You never know when they'll move on,
Life is too short for trouble and strife,
And it's too late to mourn when they're gone.

Jennifer Aston

ABSENT FRIENDS

A pillar of strength was Ned,
I cried when I heard he was dead,
One of life's props, so sadly missed,
Giving his support as we walked home pissed.

I stare at the empty rocking chair,
Where Grandma always sat,
She is resting in a new place now,
'Cos her arse has got too fat.

He died a very brave soldier,
Won a medal for what he did,
I know I'll never forget him,
'Cos the bugger owed me a quid.

Tedward

NATURE'S FRIEND

As I wander o'er the green
'Tis the prettiest sight I've ever seen.

There's the lake all quiet and still
I could never have my fill.

Ducks and moorhens, there are a few
Plus some geese, just one or two.

In due season they go to breed
Build their nests within the reed.

If you could wait for just a while
You could not help but raise a smile.

To see the lake full of new life
Ducklings, goslings, moors are rife.

And as you watch the setting sun
Once more nature's course is run.

Another day comes to an end
So it's home we go my friend.

As I depart I shed a tear
But look forward to next year.

When once again I wander o'er the green
To the prettiest sight I've ever seen.

Chas Dainty

MY FRIEND

Walk paths together even though we're apart
My friend, I love you with all of my heart
Together we've struggled with laughter and tears
Together we conquered all oncoming fears

In childhood we grew, played games side by side
With honest emotions, we had nothing to hide
In teens, you were there to comfort me too
My heart had been broken, first love had flown through

As adults we faced life full in the face
Hand in hand we could make it, with God's given grace
The mountains we climbed, echoing sadness but hope
With each other to cling to, there was no slippery slope

Together we found our life partners to love
So special, it must have been from heaven above
Our babies were born, a sweet girl and a lad
We were parents - that's something we both never had

You made me laugh, I made you smile
With tears in our eyes, I held you awhile
A new life had called you, a life overseas
Yet nothing could part us, no, not you and me

That bond it still binds despite all the miles
The bundle of letters, the photos, the smiles
No words can express, you're still my best friend
Now and for always, right through to the end

Teresa Wilson

BLUE

I see you in my *heart's eye* every day
Always there - so close though far away.
The times we shared, the laughs, the sadness too,
Were oh so much better - because of you.

Your kindly care for others and for me,
Your determination in adversity,
And when my life's purpose seemed all gone
Your strength a rock for me to lean upon.

Although the long miles separate us still
It makes each meeting short with sweetness fill,
And with the love that you, dear friend, display
Gives me a lasting treasure here to stay.

Angela Hamer

LASTING FRIENDSHIP

We've been friends for many years
Lots of joys and many tears
Partners gone and children grown
Now we face life all alone.
But contact with a friend so dear
By 'phone or letter, bring us near,
In summer time we travel too,
On holiday our ties renew.
Though far apart as is out lot,
Our lives diverse, it matters not.
Family problems shared as well,
What of the future - who can tell?
But what I do know in my heart
Is she's my friend, though far apart.

Marjorie H Smith

GOODNIGHT DEAR FRIENDS

Oh me, oh my, how time does fly like birds away
Fast winging now into the arms of yesterday
We've played and sung sweet melodies both old and new
A tapestry of harmony woven anew.

You've listened well, you've all been swell, so pleased are we:
We won't forget the pleasure of your company
We've raised a glass, and drunk the health of dear old friends:
We have tonight, no matter how tomorrow ends.

We'll come again on future date to entertain
We hope that you will come and hear each sweet refrain:
So may we say with silver strings 'Goodnight, God bless
May dreams be filled with melodies of peacefulness.

Goodnight, goodnight - goodnight, goodnight, dear friends, goodnight:
We hope you've made a memory to shine so bright
So wish us well, and pray that we both night and day
May seek and find more golden songs to sing and play.

Violet M Corlett

WHERE ARE YOU NOW?

Where are you now, the friends we once knew
You know we said we would never be blue,
We'd smile whatever came along
We did this with a wave and a song,
Sometime later that wave was goodbye
We've never understood, really why,
Something we said, although we don't know what,
Was it what each other had, or had not,
You know how it is, holidays are great.
Then when you're home, they don't seem such mates,
So goodbye to holiday friends of the past,
Let's hope the next holiday friends will last.

Doreen Bursnell

A STRIKING OLD MAN

When grandfather first came to us
We did not know how old he was
Nor how reliable.
Regular as clockwork he wound up our day
And simply by his presence
Reminded us of things we had not done.
Not that he ever complained
And we liked him for that.
On his face you could see what time had done
And quite a lot that had defeated time.
Sometimes he unlocked his secrets -
Then we could see right through
To the frailty and simplicity
Of something that had gone on working
Through so many changes.
His voice was occasionally sharp
But we knew he was just run down
And so we would make allowances.
Adjustment was easy.
For much of the day he was quiet
And we heard him mostly at night
Breathing throughout the house
In a satisfied, old fashioned way.
When visitors came he was good:
We saw them admiring his hands -
He had a certain veneer.
In time, he was part of our lives.
The children lived by his looks.
He made us all feel at home.

Alasdair Aston

OLD FRIEND

Yorkshire born, Yorkshire bred,
For us from Lancashire that's enough said.
Sheffield steel! To Lancashire grit,
To make his life down the pits,
Of life he'd say togetherness and forgiveness,
Forgive quickly! And accept forgiveness.
       Simple words but they don't say everything!

Major Buckley signed him to make his name,
       For Notts County to make his fame.
How he loved to ballroom dance,
To leave the girls all in a trance.
The word would go round
       Tucker's back in town.

His finger now points!
To the stairway of eternal peace.
Take God's hand without any fear,
For it was him that brought you here,
He will not let you go alone,
Into the valley that's unknown.
Please take his hand!
And journey to the promised land.
A friend I will dearly miss,
Kenneth Goodnight and God bless.

Ken Pendlebury

ON THE LOSS OF A MOTHER

I've only had one real friend
And now her life is at its end,
Be it joy, and sadness too
She was there to help me through.

Help me, be it just a look
Her heart was like an open book
Never closed till God's release
Took my mother and gave her peace.

Peace from pain which brought her tears,
Peace from all life's toil and fears,
Now she lies in death's mystery
Her fingers on her rosary.

John Hampson

UNTITLED

A withering hand reaching,
towards the light of day
A power from within co-ercing with strength.
A mind fighting out against an estranged mankind.
Everyone looks,
although their eyes I cannot see.
Everyone laughs,
although a tear I can only taste.
A portrait of a beast, a voice unspoken, a sight unseen.
My beauty is within,
far beneath this strange exterior,
yet your eyes don't care to stretch that far.
For within my heart,
I feel the laughter, the crying, the humour, the heartaches.
Why am I different if I feel all your love and pain.
Don't push me aside,
don't push me away
I cannot bear to be alone,
for a friend is all I need,
let me grasp that light at the end of my day.

Lisa N Charles

NOW MY TIME IS OVER . . .

Here's to you my childhood friend
As I raise my cup to times long forgot
To gentle streams and fishing nets
To home-made kites
And railway sets.

Here's to those halcyon days
Perhaps now tinged with a rosier hue
You taught me how to roller skate
And swung with me
On garden gates.

Here's to you who led the way
And played knock-down ginger with saucy glee
We'd fight over what we should do
Then you'd hate me
And I'd hate you.

Where are you now I wonder
Do you remember things the way I do?
What of all those dreams you once had?
Has life been good?
Have you been sad?

There's one thing I'd like to change
Should I have the chance to live my life again
This time I'd like to have my friend
Not just for those precious years
But right up till the end.

If any one thing is sacred
It is the time that we all have to give
We owe it to ourselves and others
To keep in touch
With our brothers.

Marylyn Pullum

FOR A FRIEND

Take part of me with you when you go,
Please don't ask why, I really don't know.
You're part of my life that I cannot explain,
You came in from the storm to shelter from rain.
There's no sense of illusion, no need to pretend,
Your warmth and your comfort make you a true friend.
I really cannot understand - nor hope to analyse
Why you chose to be near me, I'm just not that wise.
When you came you brought with you a breath of fresh air
And yet when you leave me that will still be there.
My life I'll keep living, even when you're away
So thanks for the friendship and thanks for today.
And if you should ever come back round this way,
You'll find me no different, I'll still feel this way.
You've caused me no pain and you've caused me no sorrow
But because of your strength, I can face my tomorrow.
So what can I give you; I truly don't know
But remember me sometimes, if ever you're low.
Think back to the evenings, those few stolen hours
When no-one else mattered; they'll always be ours.
And wherever you go, and whatever you do,
May your goals be achieved and your dreams all come true.
I'll not envy you ever your freedom to roam,
But I'll stay in the warmth of my safe, stable home.
There's part of me missing but for that I'll not yearn
You've given me more, much more in return.
So happiness to you, there'll be no regret;
I'm a much better person since the day that we met.

Sheila Cook

FRIENDSHIP

How glad I am to speak and wonder
To dance where wild bluebells grow
Of all the things you mean to me
All four seasons are a'glow

Has it kept? our Costa Brava
Draining colour, befriended time
When we bicycled together
Lost in laughter, French red wine

For what purpose do we stand
Support and love, a helping hand
The clothes we share and things we borrow
A need is there through times of sorrow

Still however hard we try
There's always dreams that fail and die
Little fields with boulders dotted
Grey stone shoulders, saffron spotted

Whatever problems arouse and follow
Together we shall find tomorrow

Elizabeth Petrie

LIFE LONG FRIENDS

I know I'll never find a friend,
Unlike any other.
She was with me many years,
My dear departed mother.

As I look through bags of photos,
Fond memories come to mind.
Of seaside trips, and family days,
Again, I'll never find.

She led me through my school days
Teenage problems, she would bare,
Then when I had my family,
She would still be there.

If just one wish be granted,
I know what it would be
To have my life long friend again,
Here beside of me.

Pamela Mitchell

THE GOLDEN YEARS

The war is over, some men died.
Many hearts broken, many cried.
But one came through a soldier proud.
Head held high amongst the crowd.
He found his sweetheart waiting there,
She still loved him she still cared.
Down the aisle they did glide,
Holding each others hand with pride.
As their love and happiness progressed,
They decided to start afresh.
So across the water they did go,
New pastures and new seeds to sow.
The family grow, the years do pass,
The links with home are still held fast.
Amidst the happiness and tears,
They've now been married fifty years.
Now they're back here to spend
Some time with family and friends.
Back to the old country great,
So that we can celebrate
With them, on this anniversary
Of fifty golden years!

S Heaven

FRIENDSHIP NOW DISTANT

Oh dear friend what is wrong with thee
Pick me up one day, or no memory
Of all those times we had close contact
Latter years and days gone by, that is fact

Our first days together, and seventeen
Work came second, to hell with routine
To others we were different and strange
Our past of hardship, friendship was made

Then one day I left, you felt very alone
Somehow you managed and often phoned
You moved away to try something new
Alone and knowing no-one, except Sue

Often at weekends, I would come and stay
From East-End to Pinner, pleased to get away
Your home like a mansion, but plenty to do
Children to care for, lots of domestic too

A job you enjoyed, but it all got too much
So returned home to familiarities in a rush
By that time I could drive, very convenient
To visit you at times of low and discontent

Destined we were to meet our boyfriends
Yours more serious, my heart on the mend
No more visits, and phone calls to be
Now I was alone and no friend to visit me

Years gone by we've both settled down
Your life has changed more I've found
Less time for friends who never forgot
When you needed someone, fear not

Susan Eason

FRIENDSHIP

Friendship is about you or me
Gathering round some pubs you see
We all get together all people we know
When we're all feeling somewhat low.

We talk about what we all do
And meet at different places too
Have a few beers, shorts as well
And seeing what we have to tell.

We meet about just once a week
But some we do just have to seek
It's fun, it's nice, it's really great
We have a laugh on those who's late

We care about what we all do
We try and help each other too
We wave to people outside the door
Giving to people, giving to the poor.

Friendship is what we all know
Helping people when they get low
Being there when they're upset
Not letting on and in a fret.

We take our time, and see them all
We have a laugh and have a ball
Friends are there to see you play
And that's how we enjoy our day.

Wendy Colbert

MORE THAN JUST A FRIEND

I was hungry, you held food to my mouth
I was cold, you gave me warmth.
I was doomed, you gave me a chance. I had
                nothing to give to you

You saved me from the life I had, or rather the
                life I didn't have
I existed, I drew breath, but I wasn't living.
Like a flower in the spring, you came to me.
It was than that I remembered how beautiful
                flowers really are.

Like a lighthouse in the ocean, you watch over me.
Only now do I remember how wonderful the
                ocean can be.
You shared my sorrows and helped me to love
Myself. I could offer you nothing.

Friend is such a common title, a kind of happiness
                that I'd never dreamed of.
I'm happy now. I have my life back, I'm living
I'm living in the hope that one day I can do something
For you, but all you ask is that I be your friend,
But I don't have to answer that, and you don't need to ask.

Bonny Metin

FOR RICKY

Dad's in uniform, inspecting the troops;
Clash of tarmac 'neath their hob-nail boots.
Us in uniform, chequered white and bottle green;
Never quite part of the swinging sixties scene!

Tennis racquets and football fields,
Hockey in the cold.
Who'd have thought we'd still be friends
As the child grows old.

Seventies and eighties rushed by in a whirl;
Jobs, careers, husbands and a little girl.
Telephone calls, railway stations, letters crossing in the post.
Who'd have thought we'd still be friends as the child grows old.

Now we're stepping through the nineties -
Not quite sure what we've to do
But who'd have thought we'd still be friends -
The child, that's me and you.

Margaret Stevens

HELGA

Do you remember the early days
at Barcelona University?
We were students eager to exchange
two foreign languages and a friendship.
It has survived the test of time.
Twins in learning zeal we made a pledge,
if we did not marry, later in life
we would not let anyone stop us
from seeing the world.
We'll travel together, we said,
visiting Venice and Rome
and anywhere else our fancy takes us.
But we did marry and lived life to the full,
tasting the bitter and the sweet.
Forty years on and time has not passed in vain,
we both have had our share of everything.
Now, both close two retirement age,
and in spite of living far away from one another
we are still hoping and planning ahead,
to meet at the end of the day
when you are 60 and celebrate your birthday!

Jacqueline Gonzalez-Marina

MY SPANISH FRIEND

It was three months ago we met.
Instantly, it was indisputable
We would immediately click.
His chestnut, sun-bathed face stood out
Among the pale ones surrounding him.
His personality shone through
His flawless complexion,
And his love of life was obvious
By his permanent smiling face.
His wild black locks of hair
Seemed uncontrollably carefree,
Yet added to his unique individuality.
His large enchanting brown eyes
Waited to be explored.
Nothing seemed to disillusion him,
His foreign origin was visible
By his slight Spanish accent.
We said very little
But, the little we did say
Meant so very much.
Although, during his short stay
We were unable to get to know one another
As much as I'd have liked,
Our friendship has flourished through letters.
Three months have now passed,
It's evident that our friendship,
Will stand the test of time.

Shabnam Walji

FOR GLAD

How should I write these words to you dear friend
When I have only known the briefest touch
Of mind to mind, yet snatched a glimpse of soul
To feel the warm affinity of such?

There is no call to share each other's needs,
Our paths cross not the same time-measured way.
How then might I express my view of one
Whose exit meets the starting of my day?

A fleeting vision then! A passing flame,
Your presence felt more surely for its glow
Which offers to the world a quiet compassion,
A silent comfort whither it may go.

No summer sun has ever shone so bright
As when your lovely face reflects a smile,
And I have seen it cast a net of wonder -
A magic for those caught within its spell.

Now as the evening's air comes softly drifting
To lend its coolness to the lonely skies,
I sense a strange, sad sighing up above me
As heaven's stars feel envy for your eyes.

Don't ever lose your gentle tender nature
For love is needed in the world today
God planted you to magnify a gesture,
A special sign for showing each His way

Patricia Samuels

DEAR DAD

Old friend, we have lived many good times and bad,
We have walked and talked, played games together,
At times I've not understood your ways and needs,
And I know we have both felt pain and pleasure.

But as we've grown older and the years pass by,
I have not forgotten the love and work you did,
To give me childhood memories of happy times,
Birthdays, Christmas's, holidays as a kid.

Your hair now silver barely covers your head,
And you walk at a speed much slower than mine.
And sit and talk about the good old days,
Life changes so much with the passage of time.

I hate the years that have stolen your strength,
You were always my hero, strong and brave,
And I worry each day as our lives go by,
That I'll never repay the love you gave.

There's nothing I can do to slow our lives down,
But hold on tight to good times we've had,
And I regret the moments I should have said,
I love you, I need you, you're special, my Dad!

Richard Lowis

A VALEDICTION

You will darken my life with your leaving,
As you go hopefully to the turrets of brightness,
To live with the silks and the splendour
And the colours of your imagination
For me all will be as before.
Each day following its fellow,
Too ordered to be even dull.

But at least I have been with you,
Though I never possessed you in any acceptable way.
The strands which you will weave
Into the brilliant patterns of your tapestry
I will have fingered and felt
Their warm satin texture.
I alone will understand how the picture is composed,
And sometimes in the sameness of my life,
Will fall, as your parting gift to me,
A faint rainbow of remembrance.

Valerie Skinner

WE'LL MAKE IT

I'd almost forgotten the pain
Thankfully, a brighter, lighter way,
Of going with the flow of life,
And then sadly, suddenly,
All the hurt comes creeping back
Hurry, forsake, don't let it.
Get a grip and keep hold tight
Look in the eyes and feel the stare
Get off on it and laugh, laugh
Hugging will heal the hurt
Existence will be fun with
Me and thee, them and us
Steady and safe, secure as buildings
Keep up the hard, rewarding moves
See it and so, full steam ahead
We'll handle it all, if only, we will
Not to have fears, be strong, no doubts,
Be sure, all the way, along the line
Don't, won't let it be taken away
Love for us, for them, for you and me.

Stiggy Zeum

MRS EILEEN DAVIES

First she moved to Scotland and now Australia's sunny climes
And it is difficult to phone her with the difference in time
Still, we keep the letters coming at least one a week
She from the land of kangaroos, I from the land of leeks
There is twenty five years difference in our age but that matters not
When we first me, it was amazing the many shared interests we've got
We may only get together now by phone or by the pen
What difference does it make, Eileen will always be my friend.

Melanie M Burgess

FRIENDSHIPS THAT HAVE STOOD THE TEST OF TIME

Elizabeth my dear friend
For thirty years were written
We have stood the test of time and distance.
We have grown families
In beautiful Waterford, Ireland you've lived.
God has blessed us, loving husbands and children have we
Happy memories of the past
And of our friendship to last
In London we were born
But seen many a countryside dawn
Many years I've walked with our dog
King, pass countryside and streams
Our puppy Killian will walk the same road
As I tell him about King
May mankind love animals, for they
               give us love dearly
Clearly one day Elizabeth we'll meet
It will surely be a treat, we'll talk of years passed.
And how we will *laugh* many happy more years dear friend.

Catherine Stanton

SPECIAL FRIENDS

It's not long ago when we walked hand in hand
Along miles and miles of golden sand
Dreaming what we'd be when we grew older
Looking back now, I wish I'd been bolder.

We were best friends, I loved you so much
My heart would melt at your mere touch
But you only saw me as a friend
I wished my time with you would never end

You'd rush to tell me about your latest boy
You were like a kid with a new toy
Then one day you came to me so breathless and bright
And in just a few seconds you put out my light

On your left hand you flashed a sparkling ring
Be happy for me - I'm getting married, you started to sing
I've never seen that look in your eyes before
I can't stop the tears falling as you close the door.

The big day has now come at last
I stand in the church, but my mind's in the past
In the days of walking hand in hand
Along miles and miles of golden sand.

A R Potter

A DISTANT VOICE

A distant voice echoes in sound
Not seen but heard
Not seen but felt;
Through passing of time
It's strength only grows
Never diminished at all,
My heart clearly knows.

Neil Blackshaw

TIME, SEA OR LAND

No amount of land or sea,
Could keep best friends apart.
Nor can years of separation
Sever the ties of the heart.
Together forever no matter how far
true friends will always be
Two thousand miles is too far for some
but not for you and me
We'd write to share our joys and woes
and ring just to say hello
A good friend is always there for you
No matter where you go
And when after years of being apart
two friends walk hand in hand
We proved that friendship can't be broke
by time or sea or land.

M Whitehead

FARAWAY PLACES
(Dedicated to Anna)

I have a friend of many years,
We've shared both laughter and many tears
She's helped me out when I've been in arrears
I miss her, now we live so far apart,
Not even the distance makes our friendship depart.
I love her with all of my heart.
I look forward to the postman's call
All of a sudden I'm having a ball.
They say absence makes the heart grow fonder,
In actual fact - It just makes the pain grow stronger.

Mercedes Jordan

A TREASURED FRIENDSHIP

I treasure your friendship
In each and every way
Like flowers in the meadow
You brighten up each day

I treasure your friendship
the things that you do
My life would be poorer
If it was lived without you

I treasure your friendship
The kindness you show
By ignoring my mistakes
And encouraging me so

I treasure your friendship
We have something so rare
A special kind of love
And hearts that really care

I treasure your friendship
There's nothing else as bold
It will stand the test of time
And last until we're old

I treasure your friendship
And pray that God will bless
Each day of your life
With peace and happiness.

Kay Holmes

ABSENT FRIENDS

To step together on an unknown path
Amidst a rocky and twisting way
Although it is alive we are,
To see a smile and clasp a hand
                      another day
We remember it well, a joke
          a raucous laugh, by a
                    campside fire, the steaming
Water can for tea, toasted
Sandwich smoked, the last
Cigarette cut in half.
Yes we remember it well out
At night on a duckboard worn
With trodden boot, and weathered
Frail, where a shell-holed body
Could not be found without a light.
Companionship and faith are
Firmly based in troubled times.
Some are left in distant shores,
But are forgotten not,
They are there with a part of us
And can never be taken
         from our minds!

Norman Letts

SATURDAY THOUGHTS

Fill up my time for now a friend is gone,
Commanding, demanding: of latter years quite worn
But still the spark was there of life expectancy
Of interest in the world and duty shed reluctantly
Each detail life's minutae performed so perfectly

O Abso-bally-lutely!

Love of life's memories sustained her well
And laughter before life's jester rang his bell
And then, how strange, a quiet acceptance of life's end.
So Annelaine, no more the talk and strong debate
For you have gone, my friend.

Audrey Roberts

GONE FOREVER

There is distance between us now,
And sometimes I feel so alone,
Alone with my thoughts
Alone as never before
He went because he said he had to go,
But why not with me, why alone,
Alone to a far off place,
A place of unfamiliar faces, unfamiliar people,
A place of peace and quiet, 'A place to think,' he said

The space between us now is great,
Like a deep uncrossable void,
Where there is no sound.
Where dreams and thoughts lie hidden,
If only I could cross that void.
And bring out my thoughts and tell him of my love,
A love that has even lasted the test of time

We that were so close, are not just friends,
He that meant everything to me, now lost forever,
A kiss, a touch is not just a breath of wind,
On the ocean of time,
Just a time to think, to feel,
A love that lasts forever,
Is now just a thought for an absent friend.

Hazel Webb

FRIEND

Will you be my friend for life.
Loyal, trustworthy, but not a wife.
Be there for me, show me you care.
Listen to problems, always be there.
Hold me when needed, be strong when you must.
Show strength in your love, don't misplace our trust.
I can offer you devotion, with patience and need,
Kind words written down for you always to read.
A shoulder to cry on when times become bad,
Bring happiness and joy, when you're feeling sad.
As friends show our love of each others mind,
Pass over faults that others will find.
Look at the person that is hidden within,
Then maybe a friendship for life will begin.

Steve Clarke

SILENT THOUGHTS

Fill your glass and have a care
For friends and family no longer there
Christmas seasons been and gone
Undisturbed they slumber on
But our memories very clear
To us they're still sitting here
In our minds eye, they'll always be
Fresh and gay and part of me
Although bright eyes have closed
And voices we loved are still
And their bodies now dust
On the side of a lonely hill
But we can see them anytime
In our silent thoughts at will.

Winifred Wardle

FRIEND

I feel your pain, in the death of your friend
How you suffer inside at his tragic end
The time you gave to help him through
When addiction called, you told him true
As you held his hand through his despair
You couldn't get into his mind to care
For the depth of sadness not understood
He couldn't share as you thought he should,
You asked me to pray for you and your friend
I tried so hard to soften and lend
You my arms to cry your tears
And a place to rest from your lonely fears.

Trish Birtill

A FRIEND

Should you find a friend one day
As you go along your way,
I find that friends are very few
And really not so very true.

A friend in need is one indeed
So the proverb says for us to read.
But this is not always true to say.
When you're lonely and need to pray.

You find that kindness is a guide
And a friend is on your side.
There's someone who you can confide,
Someone to trust nothing to hide.

So should a friend once let your down
Don't go around wearing a frown
Lift your heart try to forget
And just pretend you ever met.

Barbara Ward

UNTITLED

As two young girls skipped home one day
We never guessed one would move miles away.
Our friendship put to the test
One in Canada the other one left behind
Now 49 and 51 our letters have
Flown back and forth for 40 years,
Sharing moments of laughter and
Moments of tears.
Those moody teens, our marriages
Our sons and daughters' births
Our pain and agony of our middle-aged girth.
This year our sons left the nest
Leaving us Jackie, Ken, Linda and
Henry, some say to enjoy the best.
As I await my third grandchild
Jackie I will tell you what precious
Little people these are.
And I will send you their pictures
From afar.
Who would have thought we'd have
Kept in touch.
By letters which to us both have
Meant so much.

Linda Brabrook

FOR JOAN MARY

Friendship is precious, like fresh April showers,
Sunlight on water, and a springtime of flowers.
Lush grass in the meadows, and corn in the fields,
Walks through the heather; a shared viewpoint of dreams.

Ever present all around you; listening ears,
Arms to enfold you and drive away fears.
Never forgotten when life is no more,
For there's a tomorrow on a far distant shore.

Joan Margaret Howard

FRIENDSHIP

A friendship sacred in its grand completeness
A fellowship alike in work and prayer
A mutual confidence of wondrous sweetness
A love transforming every passing care
A season when the wonders of creation
Unfold such beauties unperceived before
When hopes and aims gain fuller inspirations
And life seemed crowned with joy evermore

And then an intervening shadow stealing
Like chilling mists beneath the darkened sky
A sense of growing coldness altered feelings
A restless longing nought can satisfy
A friendship that exists in memory only
An agony of silent mental pain
A saddened life grown wearisome and lonely
A radiance dimmed that cannot shine again

And yet perchance in God's own bright forever
That future life mysterious and vast
Those aching hearts whom more than distance sever
Shall meet in perfect sympathy at last
And in that union ever closer growing
Where nought of earth or heaven can divide
Will find their cup of gladness overflowing
Which God by grief and loss hath sanctified.

R D Hiscoke

THOUGHTS OF YOU

If absence makes the heart
      Grow fonder, mine is
            Fonder still,
Just thinking of the happy
      times we spent together,
           Will
Forever be, just close to me
      As thoughts are precious
           Too,
Dreams disappear at break
      Of day, but memories
           Stay of you.

E T Usher

OVERSEAS

When I see a poppy
Blowing in the breeze
I think of all the graves I saw
When I went overseas.

I stood in one small corner
With my hand upon my brow
I wondered where you died
I also wondered how.

You were fighting for your country
With bayonet and gun.
Fighting for your family
Your daughter and your son.

I never would have known it
I never would agree
That I was going to lose you
Fighting overseas.

Francesca Holmes

DO NOT WEEP AT MY GRAVE

Do not stand at my grave and weep
I am not there, I do not sleep.
I am the countless winds that blow,
The diamond glints on virgin snow.

I am the Lark's song in a sky of blue,
Gentle autumn rain caressing you.
I am lush green fields where grazing sheep,
With sad-eyed cows lie down to sleep.

I am rolling hills and soft green dales,
Meandering rivers, where life prevails.
The sound of church bells across frozen field,
Heralding Christmas joy with successive peal

I am the cat so wrapped in fur
Whose rhythmic and appreciative 'purr'
Succumbs to slumber, secure on your lap,
Dream on dear feline - enjoy your nap.

I am the robin on winter's morn,
A shaft of sunlight on ripening corn,
I am autumn leaves descending in brown and gold,
To carpet the earth in soft rich mould.

I am the flight of a gull o'er a stormy sea;
This is how to remember me!
So do not stand at my grave and cry
I am not there - I did not die

Mungo

SO MANY GOODBYES

First there was Gwyneth, with her *real gold* hair
and Angela with ten-years-old style and flair.
But it was goodbye to them and *so long to you.'*
as we moved on, seeking a different view.

Then there was Sandra, we read books we didn't ought to
and Lisa; well-spoken; councillor's daughter.
So many friends, so many goodbyes.
'We're moving again. Now wipe those tears from your eyes.'

Two hundred miles from the hills of Wales
to just within sight of the Derbyshire Dales.
This time my accent built barriers so high
friendless; at night alone I'd cry.

But like all nomads I learned to adapt
'til finally they came to accept
me; a little highly-strung, easy to hurt,
always untidy in my un-ironed skirt.

I've lost touch with them all over the years
and yet, I haven't moved since, I'm still here.
Perhaps I don't know how to stay friends for long
after so many years of moving on.

Do they ever think of me, their absent friend?
Or were *their* hearts quicker to mend?
Surrounded by friends but lonely and cursed
surrounded by water, but dying of thirst.

If I'd fed these friendships, prepared for the drought
I'd have had sustenance in times of doubt.
So many friends, so many unwritten letters
so many promises to visit when the weather's better.

Where did all the years go? The years of loneliness and pain?
Is it too late now, to find a friend again?

Sally Quilford

FRIENDS

This is what friendship means to me . . .
Whether it's two five or three
Having your there when times are hard
Making me feel you're my guard
Helping me through all that's bad
To see your faces makes me glad.

And when we all stand by, together
This gives it strength to last forever
There are so many memories
Collected on the way
That you've all contributed
To brighten up my day
You can wipe away my pain
Make me laugh throughout the rain
Bring out the sun, throughout the night
Smother the blackness with your light.

We've had some laughs
Looking back at the silly things we've done
I guess we're not the *norm*
But by God, we've had some fun
We are at times a rather motley crew
But all that really counts to me
Is that life is filled with you.

I'm glad to have you for my friends
To me this means a lot
We're like a special family
And all we have, we've got
This is something you can't beat
Friendship is . . .
What makes my life complete.

Mandy Southern

FRIENDS

How wonderful it is to me
To invite friends round for tea,
To talk about this and that,
The kids, the dog, the house, the cat,
And even if it's been some time
Since I have seen these friends of mine,
It only seems as yesterday
That we last met along the way.
Since we last chatted gleefully
And parted, sadly, tearfully.
It's been ten years since last we met
But time stood still, we are friends yet,
And true to say it seems to me
We'll be friends for eternity.
True friends they say are hard to find
But I've found mine, all good and kind
I treasure each and every one
And so I shall till life is done.
They make me happy when I'm sad
And keep me steady when I'm glad
My world would be a sad, dull place
Without a friend to chat to face to face.
And even if the time's gone past
Since we last met, our friendship will last
So when we meet again for tea
We'll smile and oh, so happy be,
To talk about this and that,
The kids, the dog, the house, the cat!

Anne James

TO JOAN

Do you think we'll ever see the sun?
I can't imagine when,
The snow's been here for ages now:
Will it come back again?

It used to shine the whole day through
When I was very small,
But I think it went on somewhere else
Through the years as I grew tall.

It's oh so cold when I awake
And it's cold when I go to bed,
But I lie remembering childhood days -
The memories fill my head.

Sunsoaked walks in fields of flowers
These were some of my happiest hours,
My friend and I were free
As we skipped on velvet grass,
The sunny days seemed endless then
But soon they had to pass..

For one day she was gravely ill -
And then she slowly died,
My lovely happy childhood friend
My heart broke and I cried.
But if the sun comes back again
These memories will return,
And as the flowers start to bloom -
And the sun begins to shine,
I'll think of *Joan* and childhood days:
For these memories are - *Mine*

P Brabin

TO MAUREAN

Put your hand in the hand of God,
And despair will turn to joy.
Tell Him all your troubles -
No need to be coy!
You can bet He'll listen,
He never walks away,
He's always there, just waiting,
And He knows you pray.
He'll listen to your problems,
He'll take them all on board,
Only He, and He alone,
Knows what it affords.
Just bide your time - be patient,
Listen to His will,
He is always waiting -
For you to just 'Be Still!'
He has never left you,
He's always by your side,
He knows how much you've suffered,
He knows how much you've cried.
So just you heed this story,
And mark my words to you
God's blessed world awaits you,
I know, because it's true!

Lillian Winstanley

TRUE FRIENDS

George says he won't be my friend unless,
To the crime *he* committed *I confess*

Alice says she will be my best friend
If the cup *she* broke *I* mend

Friendship isn't something,
That should be pushed around.

Between two caring people,
Friendship can be found
Distance and time are two tests,
Which friendship must go through.
If it passes those essential tests
Your friendship must be true!

Katie Tench

THE ROSES STILL GROW

What did they do with you?
Eject you into space?
Are you in the wind,
the sea?
Are you everywhere,
are you with me?

I still answer the door to you
in my pink gingham dress
and Grandad yes, I'm still
your little princess.

In pain
you strained
to gain
that wonderful heady scent
of those dusky roses
we smelt on those evenings spent
as if in sunny climes
forgetting
the Coventry grimes.

I can still smell the roses,
I know you can too;
Their freshness remains
as my friendship of you.

Alissa Pemberton

THE TREE - FRIENDSHIP WITH NATURE

I'm shelter when it's raining,
I'm heat and comfort too,
Oft times I make sweet music,
I'm read the whole year through.

I'm not a dog though I can bark,
But silent it would be,
You may not even know my name,
But my fruit it pleases thee.

I've been with man since time began,
I've helped him cross the sea,
And from that time for food and wine,
He's always turned to me.

Fear not, I ask no favours,
But in this concrete age,
Tear not my roots asunder,
They helped you reach this stage.

A baby's cry I hear it,
I'm there in youthful spring,
Through summer and life's autumn,
And I hear the death knell ring.

So remember all you passing,
Reserve a thought for me,
Make sure I'm there tomorrow,
Your humble, faithful tree.

Joseph G Dawson

A SPECIAL BOND

Have you ever wandered what makes a true friend?
First and foremost it's on someone you can depend.
Someone always ready to lend an ear,
Bad or good news they will be pleased to hear.
A bond so strong it will never mar,
Whether you are both near or far.
Two people who can exist in a lull,
Feeling content and happy just to mull.
Over land or sea gestures show you care,
Two minds telepathically joined, forever to share.

Dawn Downie

BENJI MY BEST FRIEND

Relationships the come and go
Like the summer sun and the winter snow,
But one thing never changes me and my best friend
He's been with me throughout my life
We'll be mates to the end.
He's been with me in good times
Stuck with me through the bad.
Shared in all my happiness
A comfort when I'm sad.
He's laughed at all my rotten jokes
Talked me through my fears,
We've had a special friendship
For over thirty years.
I've had many friends in life
But to me there is no other
Than my very dearest friend of all
To me he's like a brother
I could never pay him back.
For everything I owe him
So to my best pal Benji I dedicate this poem.

Richard Leach

SOMEONE

When we were both at school you were my special friend,
all my winters were summers I thought they'd never end.
We used to go out walking through sunshine, rain and snow,
but nothing seemed to matter our lives were one long show.
We shared out all our secrets with no-one but ourselves,
we said this was our true love we were only eight years old.
We used to go on picnics, bike rides were special too,
we were stuck together nothing could part us two.
Two years passed by so quickly I couldn't believe it was true,
my special friend was leaving to another country too.
We promised we would keep in touch but of course you never do.
I wonder what he's doing now we're way past thirty-two.

Babs West

GOLDEN DAYS

A season now to gather in
the threads of dreams, of tales unspoken
to find once more those golden days
when time lay all before us.

Older now, the children grown and gone
the unaccustomed quiet yet strange to comprehend.
No childish cry to interrupt
though that in time will come
again, full circle as our lives unfold.
A breathing space perhaps to make
an affirmation of those links forged
when we were young and free.

At least with age comes understanding
no fear of rebuff would there be
but calm acceptance of life's unknown quantity.

Marjorie Springham

DRIFTING MEMORIES

As I sit alone by the waters edge my thoughts drift out to sea.
Lost in waves that calmly ebb, I think of you and me.
The times we spent together, the times we spent apart,
Are drifting past as memories that were kept close to my heart.
But as I watch them sail away, I see the sunset fade.
And tomorrow when the new day dawns, my memories turn to waves.
But that's all they can ever be, for yesterday I know,
I had to take these memories and finally let them go.
And with my new found freedom, I watch the waves pass by,
Until my thoughts finally rest, where the water meets the sky,
And in the ever changing blue, so peaceful and sincere.
I dream of future memories, whilst alone and sitting here.

Angela-Jane Norris

TO BE A FRIEND

A friendship doesn't just appear.
It's earned with love and trust,
A silent ear, a tender touch
Are all a certain must!
Someone who takes the time to care,
to listen to your woes.
To share with you the happy times,
and help you through the lows.
A friendship must work both ways,
It must be give and take.
And to expect it all one way
would be a grave mistake.
So be there for you friend,
as much as she for you.
Remember - these few words my friend
and enjoy a friendship true!

J Wells

LIVING ON MEMORIES

I'll remember everything we did together.
I'll recall the good years we had.
I'll cherish those great days forever.
I'll recollect the good times and bad.

The fun we felt, the laugh's so loud.
The pub crawls, nights out, and sunny days -
When I was content, and growing proud,
In love with you, and your lovely ways.

Seemingly my love, my life, my charm,
And meaning all the world to me.
'Twas alright, so peaceful, so calm;
Your slight caress so loving and free.

Memories of cute cuddles and a sweet kiss.
Memories of the touch of the past.
It was deep rooted, too much to miss.
A love I thought would always last.

But now you're gone, and I'm so alone,
With treasured memories only mine to keep.
Measured weepings in my lonely home
Fill my day from dawn to sleep.

My tears now fall, you hear my cries:
Recall the good times, the joy, the fun.
Cheers for the passion, the lows, the highs;
A love so vibrant, so true, so young.

But now I must look and plan ahead.
Renew my quest for the perfect friend.
Yet I'll recall all that you ever said.
Memories to comfort me until the end.

Desmond Hawthorne

LOST FRIEND

'Twas years ago we came as two,
Friends together in the dew
'Twas years ago we came together
Through the years and all bad weather

You went your way through the years
I went my way through the tears
One day we'll meet again as two
Friends together in the dew.

C J Wade

FRIENDS

Out of sorts where do you send?
Most of us to our best friend.
Eighteen years old when we met.
Taking out children or pets to the vet.
Telling each other our tales of woe.
Helped to make another day go.
Through thick and thin good and bad
A friend is a good thing to be had.
We've had our rows like cat and dog.
Making up sometimes is a slog.
Borrowing clothes or minding the kids.
Even there to lend a few quid.
Families just happen but friends you choose.
With one like mine you cannot lose.
Twenty nine years plenty of advice.
Giving and taking not counting the price.
Loved as much as a husband or wife.
A good friendship will last the whole of your life.

Catherine Spivey

THE LAST GOOD-BYE

Although we cannot see you
Your voice we cannot hear
We know that you are with us
We feel your presence near.
We think about you constantly
From morning until night
Not gone from us completely
Just merely out of sight.
It was only Springtime
When you left us on that day
The spring, it turned to summer
Then summer went away.
Soon Christmas was upon us
And then a year brand new,
The loneliest Christmas ever,
Our first one without you.
And now a year has passed
Since He came and closed your eyes
A whole year since that day
We said our last good-byes.
They say that time's a healer
When loved ones have to part
But no amount of time
Could mend this broken heart.
And as the years pass by
It may be easier to smile
You haven't gone forever Dad . . .
. . . Just left us for a while.

I miss you so much Dad
All my love always.

Jayne Watson

FRIEND

You are the oasis in the desert of my life
You are the flame in my darkness and confusion
You are the spar I cling to when I'm lost at sea
You are the warmth that keeps me alive.

You give me friendship when I'm lonely
You give me comfort when I cry
You are always there when I call
You pick me up when I fall.

You are the stars in my night time
You are the swallow in my sky
You are the waves on my shore
You are the wind beneath my wings.

Helen Ireson

PAT

When I look back over 20 years
I see a mixture of happiness and tears
But through all the good times and the bad
All the laughter and the sad.
You're the best friend I have ever had.

You helped me through the bad times
We laughed at all the good.
You're quiet a special person
I can't thank you for all I should
You love my children like your own
And make them welcome in your home

For me you've always been there
Always showed how much you care
To me you've always been a friend
I hope Pat you will be till the end

Julie Antcliff

TO ANN

Memories live forever
Our thoughts will never die
In quiet little moments
You'll often hear me cry

The smiles, the heartaches and the tears
Will stay with me throughout the years
Your funny ways, the things you said
These are the thoughts locked in my head

Stored in my heart
Those happy times and things we used to do
Every second, every minute
These thoughts are just of you

You're smile no more I'll never see
Your love, your voice, your touch
But in my heart I'll always know
I loved you very much

Because you're gone, it does not mean
You're very far away
For in good time when God decides
We'll meet again someday

A C Wilkinson

THE LOST FRIENDSHIP

We met at school, my friend and I,
We sat at desks, which seemed so high,
In parks so green, with woodland trees,
We were pirates on the high seas.

When winter came, and with it snow,
Off tobogganing, we would go,
As spring arrives, our rods we take,
We go fishing in the lake.

The years roll by, hence come the war days,
We have to go our separate ways,
Six years go by, and not a word,
I ask about my friend, no-one has heard.

One day I stand, by the Cenotaph,
A hand on my shoulder, a familiar laugh,
I turn quickly, and with a sigh,
We walk off together, my friend and I.

John G Pocklington

SEPTEMBER SUNSETS

Did you think that I'd forget you,
My family and friends?
I will never leave you again.
You're the biggest reason
For coming home I'll get.
You and September sunsets.

September sunsets
Remind me of you
Where I've come from,
And where I'm going to.
September sunsets
At the end of the day,
Are on all your faces.
And I just want to say,
How I've missed you!
You and September sunsets.

Now, the night is coming
And, the sun is going down.
Shadows wash the windows in this town.
Memories linger on,
For friends who I've met.
Leaving me September sunsets.

Paul Beretta

EVERYDAY BEST

A chubby armed hug in her little girl's room
Curled on a quilt with Berty (and Pooh)
Snug, we race to catch up with our news.

New environment, men, friends, fun.
Hold up our lives to the light, so they sparkle
The new me - improved, impressed?
She raised an eyebrow and laughs at my list,
And couldn't care less.
She's still not mine - I comment.
You'll always be my Sunday friend, she pretends, kept for best.
We stop and are (ourselves) and stare through the fast thinning rose
Missed - again.

Have I changed, do you think? My
Haven't you grown, so much, colder
Sort of hard and older, perhaps.

We were friends first, and then lovers, and thought I was
Safe, then I though that I coped, and I know it was fun it's
Just the people I've met but I guess it's gone (innocence).
I've become a predator, force, impenetrable, strong
But am I losing touch, warmth, close, peace, you?
Don't stray too far please? I can't go back
And we're everyday friends, not put on for best
In the back garden, in the sun, in the summer

I take her inside sun with me when I leave
But shield it's warmth, hold it inside, precious
So as not to melt their sparkling brightness.

Rebecca Miller

MY GOODBYE MESSAGE

You will be gone
    not long
Drifting to a place
    uncertain
New adventures,
    new friends
A place
    I don't know
I'm no part
    of your new life
Happiness at last,
    for you
A hole in life
    for me.

Jayanna Hughes

ABSENT FRIENDS

A bond is there to see
When airborne soldiers meet
Adventure, danger, happened to them and me
We survived in battle heat
To meet again in Civvy Street
The friendship grew as peace returned
and tales were told of days long past
Whenever we meet - a pint or two
It still goes on, forever to last
A bond of friendship so tight
Who fought for freedom with all their might.

So Badger Bennett and Denny Rowe
Bill Gentry, Jacko and Peat Moore
And all for fought the foe
Carry memories, strong in mind to store.

Dennis R Rowe

PASSIONATE FRIENDS

Oh my passionate friends
You will be with me until the end
You have shared my trials
And tribulations
How we would talk and talk
Into the wee small hours
Where we would build our dreams
Our heartbeats as one.

How the candle would burn
And another page would turn
As we wrote another chapter
Of this crazy life
And we would raise a glass
A glass to passions passed
And a glass to burning passions
Still to see the light

And now we are apart
But you live here in my heart
And the distance between us
Matters not at all
For the letters we write
Will keep the passions alight
Until we meet again
My passionate friends.

I Barton

THEN SHE SAID . . .

Lay me down, at the water's edge,
Whispering meadows tell no lies,
Watch the town, sleep through the night,
It's the next best thing to candle light,
Hills, valleys, rivers and trees,
Anatomy, could it be, all this natural vanity.

Then we make tracks through the grass,
Look back, trodden yellow path,
Hold hands in new found land,
And favourite flowers in the sand,
Then she said, 'Same applies -
Best friends they never die!'

Pluto Moran

PHONE FRIENDS

They lived in Acaisier Row,
Numbers ten, eleven and twelve.
They'd been friends since they were six,
All through junior school they'd chattered and giggled,
At Secondary, they discovered boys!
With make-up thick they went to discos,
And left their parents worried.
Then one of them, she moved away,
Across the sea to France.
They all ran up huge phone bills,
Their parents were so livid,
And through the groundings and phone bans,
All of them still were friends.
Now, they've got well paid jobs,
And live in different countries,
Each loves to ring the other up,
But now they pay the phone-bills.
And everyday from six till seven,
They set the phone wires tingling,
Non-stop they talk, chatter and giggle.
For this is what they are,
Three Phone Friends.

Michelle Liddle

ABSENT FRIEND

Remember all the good times
You had when you were small
The cuddles and the kisses
When you had a fall.
The laughter and the tears.
You shared all through her life,
Always there through good and bad.
Your troubles and your strife.
You think mums are forever
Then one day she's not there,
Taken from you suddenly.
Your world's full of despair
Don't take your mother for granted
Treasure her with care,
You only ever get mother
You'll miss her when she's not there.

Sandra Vickers

THE GIFT OF A FRIEND

Life has its moments of sorrow.
Its moments of pleasure and pain.
On any path we choose to travel,
May be riches to lose or to gain.
But in our darkest hour,
Or in the best that God may send.
We need not suffer or rejoice alone
When we travel with a friend
For we enter this world with nothing
And all we may ever own
Is the love that we share with others
The *greatest gift* a friend I've known

Paul Bailey

COMRADE

I know you now
and knew you then,
somehow
the years have not forgotten
that in between,
those memories rekindled
spoken anew,
no parting could ever
sever
those ties,
and so here lies
true friendship.
Through thick and thin
blood brothers we are
under the skin,
close in affection
like kith and kin,
in retrospection.

Myk Jonson

FRIENDSHIP

Fly away on a dream.
Memories calling for what might have been.
The passing of time with no looking back.
A vision of love - but what does it lack?
The substance of life and all it entails.
The passage of time with a ship in full sail.
The treasure of friendship held in your hand
As fragile as shells left on the sand.
Take care of this gift, there's none to compare
It's precious, it's sacred and ever so rare.

Alma Cooper

BEST OF FRIENDS - FOR ALWAYS

Friendship is a silken cord,
Which binds two hearts together.
And if you will not break this cord -
We shall be friends, forever.

If I choose to move away,
To some far and distant place,
That silken cord may sway.
Although my face you cannot see,
For friendship sake, remember me.

Around every corner - I will search
For that face, I'd love to see,
Because I know I'll never find, another friend,
Like you have been to me.

Victoria A Hicks

THE PRIZE OF THE WISE

The dictionary says *mutual benevolence.*
One who is loyal and will defend.
This sums up the definition.
Of what we know as a friend.

There is no written contract
Just a relationship to share.
O how we miss these comrades.
When they are no longer there.

So value those who value you.
Just for what you are.
In this world of amateurs.
To them you are a star.

T A Napper

MEMORIES OF FRIENDSHIP

She's the girl I've loved in life
She's seen me through lots of strife
When my troubles have come
And things have gone wrong
She's always been there to cheer me along
The love in her you couldn't measure
She always gives me such pleasure
And when she loves, and cares for you
She gives that love forever
She's gentle, caring, good and sweet
And to know her life through
Has been such a treat
We've had ups and down each and every day
But there's one thing dear friend,
I'd like to say,
Thank you for the love along the way.

Elizabeth Pocklington

VOW OF FRIENDSHIP

I have a special friendship
One I've always treasured
It's full of love and understanding
Its value can't be measured
Together we have formed a bond
A healthy strong alliance
Encountered problems through the years
Meeting them with defiance
Talking through the troubled times
The traumas in our life
There's nothing that we cannot face
When your best friend is your wife

Jimmy Metcalf

TRUE FRIENDSHIP

I never knew true friendship
Until you came along,
At first we wasn't really close,
But then it grew so strong.

We share so many secrets,
You know me inside out,
When you are acting strangely,
I know what it's about.

I come to you with problems,
I'm always there for you,
If we ever lost contact,
I don't know what we'd do.

We wet each others shoulders,
Crying tears of pain,
Relationships with other friends,
Have never been the same.

I've known you for five years now,
The time has gone so fast,
I just hope the next five years,
Will see our friendship last.

Donna Walton (17)

SOMETHING SPECIAL

I hope you know, you're my best friend,
Let's make it stay that way,
Until we both grow grey and old,
Until our dying day.

Although we are so far apart,
The gap is still so small,
The fact we live such separate lives
Won't affect our love at all.

We're very special to each other,
That will stay the same,
I'm always here, if there's the need,
'Cos best friends we'll remain.

Whatever happens, just remember,
We will always be,
The reason for the phrase *best friends*
It was made for you and me

Julie Swan

THE MATES I LEFT BEHIND

When I moved here from Nottingham,
        all my mates I left behind.
I remember all the fun we had,
        no better mates could you find.
The laughs and jokes we shared together,
        will stay in my mind until forever.
Every Wednesday would be coffee afternoon,
        at our children's nursery,
We'd have a drink, a laugh a gossip.
        You know her at No 63.
Then in the school yard we'd all gather,
        to collect our kids at half past three.
They would all come running into the yard,
        one would fall and graze their knee.
By the time we all finished waiting,
        we'd just about get home for tea.
I don't half miss my mates.
        maybe I'll make some new ones.
We'll have to wait and see.

P Rockley

ABSENT FRIENDS

We don't see them very often
There's so many miles away
We cannot touch or hold them
Or hear the words they say
But! We do have precious memories
Of the happy times we've known
When friendship was maturing
From the seeds of kindness sown
And when our friends are absent
It is the memories we shared
That *bridge the gap* between us
And we know how much we cared
We miss them in so many ways
And wish that they were here
But life has led them somewhere new
So this we have to *grin and bear*
But, absence ad the saying goes
Can make the heart grow stronger
And make this special friendship
More rewarding and much stronger
So here's a toast to absence friends
May God keep them in his care
And may his love just *bridge the miles*
As we remember them in prayer.

F Merrett

FRIENDS FOREVER

Despite the years that have all gone past
        I have friends who just last and last

A lucky man - I have to be
        I don't need to win the lottery

Through pain and tears - of so many years
        I've survived - I'm alive!

I'm still here at 83 - maybe 84
    And I'm still welcome at the door

Of the friends - I've known for so long
    And they listen to the songs

I play - some are old and some are new
    One or two are tinged with blue

And what do I attribute this to?
    Those friends who've stood by me
        Like You!

Harry Clarke

TO TERRY

Your eyes will never read these words but still they must be written
You thought few would mourn your passing - yet I with grief was smitten
We did not part on fondest terms and much was left unspoken
But least said soonest mended even though my heart was broken

Your troubles all are ended now and free from pain you rest
No more to face a future bleak - you meant it for the best
Your departure is respected and even understood
Bad memories will fade in time and only leave the good

Your proud and manly beauty and the wave in your fair hair
Your gentle voice and smile so brilliant even if so rare
A golden day in summer sun gathering fruit together
A six-mile walk at dead of night through cold and rainy weather

Your strength and your uncertainty - a contrast so appealing
Time spent with you though so fleeting touched my deepest feeling
I failed to be your number one however hard I tried
But wish I could have told you that my love had never died.

Mandy Smith

FRIENDS ACROSS THE SEA

It's a long time ago, I first met Joe, and Kate his bonny wife,
In a cottage small, away from it all, they lived their own sweet life.
I'd often heard of Ireland, but never thought I'd be
As a WAAF in wartime, sent across the sea.
Yet there was I at Bishops Court, a stranger to that shore
And fate it must have been that day, to be taken to the Reilley's door.
I got an Irish welcome that I never have forgot
That's where I first met Kate and Joe, and baby Eileen, in her cot.
Oh those nights besides their fire, when Joe would softly croon,
The Irish songs to the babe in his arms, as he paced around the room.
The soda-bread and tatties we ate by that fireside bright,
Must have taken most of Joe's wages, in those days, money was tight,
And to that cottage we would cycle, on most nights of the week,
Two WAAFs singing loudly, on bikes although oily, did squeak,
But those memories I have cherished of those days so long ago,
Have remained in my heart, and still deeper do grow.
Joe would know we were coming, standing outside that cottage door,
For our voices they were carried, by that soft Irish wind, that did blow,
Looking back now to those years I've seen, I am so happy to have been,
to that cottage so small away from it all
With dear Kate and Joe Reilley and their baby Eileen.

M A Atkinson

DON'T CRY TOO HARD

Don't cry too hard nor each day weep,
for I am at peace while I sleep.
I closed my eyes and found no end,
I am in the arms of a loving friend.

Don't try too hard to understand,
I now walk on our promised land.
There is no need to worry here,
my true Father holds me near.

Don't think too hard of things never done,
because I'm content my battles won.
Take my hand in your dreams tonight,
the darkness lost I've found the light.

Don't hurt too hard about words unsaid,
I sleep easy now within my bed.
Remember only our joy on a happy day,
so goodnight for now, until you pass my way.

Hazel Donnelly

MY TWO BEST FRIENDS

You could travel the world over,
    You could sail the seven seas,
    but, nowhere in the whole wide world
    were friends as great as these.

My two best friends were always there
    to lend a helping hand.
    In bad times or in sad times
    - they'd always understand.

They listened, and they tried their best
    to give me good advice.
    No matter what - they loved me,
    though I wasn't always nice.

My two best friends are gone now.
    When I think of them - I'm sad.
    For my best friends in all the world
    were called my mum and dad.

Valerie Warner

THE NIGHTINGALE

She is a friend,
Very special,
She always has a smile,
She always takes the time
to stop and talk for a while.

When times got tough,
you would hear her sing
a little tune,
and her smiling little
face, would always
wash away the gloom.

I feel quite sure
throughout my life.
I could never wish
to meet, one who
could begin such a
simple friendship.
And turn sour into sweet.

So caring, and so
giving of herself,
Sincerity, hope and trust,
what wealth!
The wealth of true
friendship
Beyond compare!

Annie Atkins

LADY

I know words cannot replace the fact that you are not here,
But how else to pass time when missing someone so dear,
I'm just trying to tell of my feelings for you,
And no-one really understands enough to talk to.
People wouldn't believe the times we had,
Mainly happy but some were sad.
Through good and bad you were there,
Someone to talk to someone to share,
Any problem big or small,
You helped me make it through it all.
I trusted in you and you in me,
A special friendship only we could see
I'm sorry it had to end this way.
But be assured of a special thought each day.
You understood me when others did not,
A loyalty that shall never be forgot.
Part of me has been broken never to mend,
That part is you my true little friend.

R Mason

MY DRINKING COMPANION

It was you who led me astray
with whispered promises of wine, women and song,
it was you who dared to open that murky door
and assured me that it was not wrong
to pick up loose girls
and not going back home
and it was you who stayed with me
when I started to fully roam
and now, after the veil of the years
have moved us both along,
I need to tell you, my friend,
that I'm glad we sung the same song.

Peter Key

TWILIGHT

When old friends gather
Old tales told, old battles fought,
Old times recalled
And youthful memories caught.

And time stands still,
Though the intervening years
Have brought their share
Of happiness, joy and tears

Years but moments
When those past times and thoughts unfold,
When old friends gather,
Old battles fought and tales are told.

Those who did not know
Nor live through that turbulent past
May not understand
Our feelings, or why they last.

The bonds were forged
And sacrifices made and yet
We still recall,
Let not the present world forget

Though some of those
Who once among us gathered here
Are not now with us,
We remember still and hold them dear

So old friends all
Mind not what the future brings,
Raise your glass to times
Of youth, of courage and braver things

Jack Pragnell

SPAN OF TIME

Ere was the span of time to that erstwhile,
Which forged so very strong the binding links;
The favour'd unity thus portrayed fulwell
O'er span of time; oh, so very true beheld -
Sincere, dear friends . . . twixt you and I.

Many are the years . . . the stretch'd miles,
But ne'er did this deter the mem'ries of;
The joys full-shared twixt we alone.
No hint of weakened stance to come, -
No stronger care than that so staunchly held!

Through fears and doubts thus well portrayed,
When first the fateful seeds were honest-sown;
To nurture that; agrowth to greater unity, has proved
By that which holds so jealously, - the truth
Of something good, that blossomed long.

'Tis memories strong that guard so very well
The swift, impinging needs of time, that seeks
In vain to ere denounce the goodly stance -
Held solid-bound, and found unwanting o'er long years,
No gilded shield could e'er outdo such task.

Be thee assured, ascattered, precious friends,
That though the distance, - time, and years subdue;
It matters-not to you or I, at all:
No greater care could e'er belie - by any guise,
The phantom-hand which reaches out to you.

Dennis F Tye

WHAT THE PASSAGE OF TIME CAN DO

There has been one great friendship that has stood the test of time - for almost an eternity.
Together, they have produced such beautiful harmony.
When either were in need, the other would lend a hand.
If tears were dripping from their eyes, they would be wiped away by the other with care.
They have danced and swayed together under trees, all over the world.
together, they brought bounteous amounts of joy to the most miserable and lonesome objects.

Now, after many years, they are in a mist of conflict,
Instead of being one; a half has decided to destroy the other.
Maybe, at first, *it* didn't intentionally want to cause damage,
It now knows the mistakes *it* has made,
Yet, *it* still makes them!
Such a shame it is to disregard the past joys and beauty that has been created.
Hopefully, it will not be long now, before *it* realises that what they once had was so special.
A friendship which can still be re-kindled, with plenty of tender loving care.
It has to wake up to one self and soon.

Man requires the earth.
They need each other to be able to love, live and flourish . . .

Tina Whelan

FRIENDSHIP SONG

A burdened heart beats free and strong
When it hears the tune of friendship's song
It lifts our spirits, makes it light
brings warmth and joy close in sight
      that's friendship's song

The heartfelt cheer, the good times many
that friendship has, there is not any
    other feeling that can bring
the inner strength that makes us sing
    the friendship song

Yes my friends I love you so and
    while we share this earth I know
That wheresoever you may go
    We shall sing our friendship song

Linda Mussett

BEN

Roaming the land in search of lust,
Causing havoc and lack of trust,
Loved by all you seemed so tame,
As wandering home you always came.
Early awakenings as you were taught,
Never seemed to pass a thought,
Never forgetting time spent together
Briskly walking all kinds of weather
Bringing great pleasure without a doubt,
Although at times there was a need to shout,
Time stands still for no man or beast
So with our lives we must feast
Growing old, but still young at heart
Missing you as life you part,
Bewildered by the light drifting aimlessly
Free from this world of wealth and treachery
Can this all but be a dream
And everlasting one it would seem
Our love for you is what we mourn
Knowing you'll never see the dawn
Man's best friend one cannot lie
    Thinking of you in purple sky.

Simon Knights

LIFE

There came a sailor boy, *so young, so gay,*
He almost stole my heart away,
The war was won, but at what cost?
His ship went down. My love was lost.

There came a *soldier boy, so clean, so smart,*
With charming ways, he won my heart.
We loved through life, with children three,
Until one day pain tore him from me.

Lastly there came a *young sailor's dad'*
We reminisce o'er the life we've had.
We share companionship, true friendship growing
Do we mind what friends say, or our neighbours knowing.

We have rides in the car, we go out to dine,
Take walks by the sea when the weather is fine.
Life's like a game, there are rules one must keep,
Respect for each other, when true friendship we seek.

Secret smiles pass between us on bowling greens,
Very often we play in opposite teams.
We share many interests, bowls, music and shows,
What's for us in the future? *Well* only God knows.

When he goes on his *cruise*, it's goodbye *sailor boy*,
For ships are his real love, his pride and his joy.;
On board there's *romance* many ladies of fashion,
Perhaps someone will arouse an old pensioner's passion.

He'll tell all the ladies he's rich and carefree!
Forgetting *past deeds*, forgetting poor me!
He'll lap up all their kisses, caresses divine,
His days will be filled with loving, whisky and wine.

When he comes down to earth from his world of fantasy,
From days spent in sunshine, nights of ecstasy,
Will he finish what he started, with eyes of navy blue,
Will he look up his *old friend* who's stayed straight and true?

V Beck

A FRIEND

How lovely it must be
To have some company
To sit in the front room, yes together

Then perhaps go out one day
To a show or just lets say
A walk a stroll in any kind of weather

It's really nice I know
To have someone you know
Who comes when things go wrong
And you don't feel right.

And if you need a friend or two
Who will know just what to do
They will always be there to help you
Day or night

Now this isn't just a rhyme
Or something to pass the time
I'm sure you understand just what I'm saying

I'm really quite sincere
So please don't shed a tear
Yes please just come around here
That's what I'm saying.

Jean Skates

THE MEETING PLACE

So often I still walk
Where once we were together
Where we would daily talk
In minl or cruel weather,
Where we would come to say
The solemn words and wise,
Where I would see each day
The love shine in your eyes.
So often I still wait
Where light my steps were going,
When I was always late
On morn when it was snowing,
Where daily you would be
To open great Church door,
And I would come to see
Your shining eyes once more:
So often I am by
The pews where we were kneeling,
To pray to God on high
With heartfelt love and feeling.
So often I am near
The birthplace of our meeting,
And pray that I may hear
From you the words of greeting;
But heart feels only pain
And tears run down my face,
As I yearn yet again
To see you in this place.

Lily Jakubowski

REMEMBER

Remember the fun we had at school
        Lots of laughs - we had a ball!
Remember you'd come to ours for tea
        And how you'd make eyes at me brother Lee!
Remember my nerves on my very first date.
        Then I fixed you up with Dave's spotty mate
Remember you were mad that night
        We had our one and only fight
Remember times staggering back from the Crown
        And our Friday nights out on the town
Remember our first jobs down the market
        Your first car and the trouble to park it!
Remember you got married first
        I really thought my heart would burst
Remember thinking we'd lose touch
        But you told me you loved me far too much,
Remember my fling with Barry Blake
        Then nine month's later - Baby Jake!
Remember him calling me a tart
        He walked away and broke my heart
Remember how only you were there
        When life was sometime hard to bear
Remember you gave me your spare bed
        But what went wrong - I lost my head
Remember your pain when you found out
        Me and your Mark'd been playing about
Remember I saw the pain in your eyes
        You couldn't believe our friendship was lies
Remembering back I feel so sad
        For I've lost the best friend I ever had . . .

Jacqueline M Arkell

TO THE NEXT THIRTY YEARS

At five years old we shyly smiled
Our first school day all strange and new
A friendship forged from that day on
Complete with tears and laughter too!

A different class at Junior School
Meant that we were soon apart
But we would be together soon
I knew that in my heart.

We were together again at Senior School
Working hard (well, sometimes anyway!)
Taking exams before leaving for good
We looked forward to that day

We worked side by side for many years
Earning money and having fun.
Boys and money came and went
But we remained as one.

The time came at last to settle down
With mortgages and men.
But through it all we knew we'd be
The same as we were then.

Now we are wives with children
Who feel the way we do.
That friendship should last a lifetime
Complete with tears and laughter too!

Anne Greatorex

MAYE IN THE KILLING FIELDS

A ball of golden star dust
Maye in an African marigold Easter bonnet of loveliness
Fecundity in a freshly made marriage bed,
Promising the potential of gifted sons and lovers
And a DNA strand of grandchildren embolden to love.

I roll a ball of dust in my dancing hands;
Hanging out our prayer of Sunday washing under a dishcloth winter's sky
Answering urgent phone calls from who - Mary
Ministering angel to Alfie and Ivy's shocked needs
Spiking their surprise tea with whisky and rye irony.
Now marooned at the Cross Inn at our waves parting.
Writing your last footings in careful lace.
With blood money from my own parents wake.
Planting a fine tree for Ivy and the irony of men.

I light the bowl of fire in praise of other mothers.
Your eyes will forever be the colours of the North Sea.
Now I celebrate your departure in a balloon port glass;
Drinking a long lass to the longevity of humanity.
Fulfilled in your illuminated halo rolling over the Lincolnshire Wolds
In your decay is our awakening - Maye adorned in Eventide shrouds.

You are now transformed
In acquiring your kingfisher soul in the resurrected sun.
In the rim of your beginning - begetting Maye in playful spray
On Mablethorpe's eternal sands - Om! Om! Om! - under a big sky
Wavelengths - oyster catcher - flashbacks curving the North Sea
Now on my raft in death - from within I swim.
In your long hot summers in Thor's wondrous waters.
Maye now glancing heavens fields - agape
        In that sea of revelations.

Reuben Crowe

MY LIFE LONG LOVE

Ah yes, you know me best -
The hidden contours,
And the unspoken tongue
Of my soul
Are not alien to you . . .

You move within my realms
With careful tread.
I feel your thoughts,
Your mind, your love
We belong one to the other . . .

Long ago, when we were young
You held my hand
And stole my heart.
Custodian of all my life,
I gladly gave you all . . .

So now 'tis ours, this path well-trod
Ourselves closely weaved
Though our chances were scorned
By those long ago
Who said we'd never last . . .

My life, my love are all for you.
I desire no more
I need no more
My life-long friend -
The man I wed . . .

Julie Parkinson

A NEED TO GROW

I still pass the old house sometimes
The one you used to live in
Back in those old, innocent days
Or so they seem now
Ah, but it's not the same anymore

And the wind still chills sometimes
Outside the house where you lived
And the room where we had those parties
Still has the same curtains
Ah, but it's not the same anymore

Because you flew away to somewhere new
Somewhere distant where people like you can grow
Because dreams are so easily crushed round here
Yet I was just like you, I had a need to grow
Oh, why didn't you take me with you?

And the air round here grows thinner every day
More dreams die as the flowers do
You were the lucky one, who ran away
And my jealousy can't kill my admiration
Oh, but why couldn't you take me with you?

I still pass the old house all the time
The one we used to dream in
And although you're now gone
You're still the best friend I ever had
Ah, but it's not the same anymore

Damian Green

MY PATERNAL FRIEND

Into the world I came,
the innocent little girl.
This bundle you'd help make,
this bond would never break

A child in your arms,
my special little place.
Safe in your protection,
wrapped in warm affection.

Drifting from your arms
to grow in my own mind,
you still watched over me,
your face I'd always see.

Through the troubled times
life placed in our path,
you'd try to understand,
be there to hold me hand.

Boyfriends filled my life,
but no-one could compare.
Our love will never end,
my dad, my special friend.

Shelley Brown

HEARTS APART

I write this letter to you,
    As my heart is at a low,
You wished to stay here with me,
    But we knew you had to go.

The time will pass, like before,
    And you'll return again,
Your smiling face, bringing sun
    To replace my inner rain.

My thoughts are always of you,
    Each night as I go to bed,
Each morning when I awake,
    You're still there in my head.

May God return you safe to me,
    And watch over you 'til then,
No ink has written these words,
    It's love flowing from my pen.

Duncan Callander

FOREVER FRIENDS

Sun sets and this the final time
Truth discards its claim
Once eternal friendship sleeps
And nothing heals the pain

Two separate and two silent lives
No words to smile and share
Unable to believe in fate
Life drifts unseen to care

Held within, once certain dreams
This time we could not khow
As life can disregard our needs
And the hurt we cannot show

With final prayers, unending verse
We turn to face the sun
Resting from a search for peace
Our journey ends as one

Sharon Foot

FOREVER MY FRIEND

How do you describe a friend,
It's an easy word to say.
But true friendship is something which
Matures with time, as if ripening
From day to day.
A true friend knows when you feel
Empty afraid or alone.
They can brighten your day or thoughts
With words from their hearts so
Cherished, and to you so clearly shown.
I've had this special friend with
Me for many a year now. But it
Wasn't until I spoke out and asked
For his guidance that I realised I
Would never have to be alone.
I know he will always be there
And walking by my side.
And when I speak of him to others
He is a friend to speak of with
Great pride.
Ours is a friendship that will never
Fade, and more and more I feel
His love. If we all could
Open our hearts we could all
Share this wonderful friendship
Of our dear Lord in the Heavens above.

Dian

TO CHOOSE A FRIEND

Some people always seem to have,
A shoulder for you to cry on,
They always sit and listen,
They're someone you can rely on.

They always make you smile,
No matter how you feel.
With patience and understanding,
Their concern proves to be real.

You share the same sense of humour,
You laugh at things together,
Sometimes you sit and wonder,
Just if they've been around forever.

The silence you share is comforting,
Each memory you have, they're in,
You can't really seem to recall,
When this friendship did begin.

No matter how far apart you've been,
The miles always seem to be few,
It's never too much trouble to call,
Just to see if there's anything new.

You've shared happy times and sad times,
You can't count what you've been through,
These are true values of friendship,
Values that I see in you.

Elaine Gisbourne

WHEN THE BLACKBIRDS SING

The long hand strikes, it's 12 o'clock,
the emotions break, a smile and tear,
and I propose a toast to you,
so sorry that, you aren't here.

A good friend, you have been to me,
on this New Year's Day, so far away;
trying to break oppression free,
and bring an entire nation a brighter day.

I think of you on a foreign shore,
glancing over the waters longingly,
yet, it wasn't you that caused this war,
that has parted you from family.

But, you so adamant in career,
to serve the Queen, and bide her call,
never mind, when you're home we'll have a beer,
then you can tell us about it all.

Yet you decided on the infantry,
to make this world a safer place,
and confront head on, all tyranny,
true guardian of the human race.

I think proudly of you, and raise this glass,
lonely in your errand of peace,
and quietly watch the midnight pass,
forever may all conflict cease.

But, we'll wait until your duty's over,
and celebrate New Year in the spring,
when the lapwing wheels above the clover,
and the happy blackbirds start to sing.

Derek Atkinson

THE ALBUM

Remember our first school photograph
as we sat with neatly crossed limbs.
It always made us really laugh,
those tight lipped ear to ear grins.

That's you and I in the garden
playing with the neighbours' cat.
We tried to put him in a doll's pram,
he never came near after that.

Here is one of us in our teens,
arm in arm on Blackpool prom,
savouring vanilla ice-cream,
with *Kiss me Quick* hats on.

This was your wedding invitation
with two horseshoes entwined.
That's a squashed cake decoration,
can't tell if it's yours or mine.

You are here expecting your first born.
This was the Christening affair.
On here we're a little well worn,
matured signs of grey in our hair.

It's nice to flick open the pages,
to sit, look back and laugh.
Going through life in each stages.
Oh! just one missing photograph.

Now dear friend, please don't worry.
The empty space with a tacky mass
is where I peeled one out in a hurry
to stick on my Pensioners' Bus Pass.

Linda Hunter

GONE BUT NOT FORGOTTEN

The need to talk,
The need to share,
The need for you is always there

To pick up the phone,
To scribble a note,
Now you are gone, my heart is broke.

At 2 am I'll want to call;
Confess my sins,
And tell you all!

Not so easy now though.
Too difficult by far.
I'll no longer find you up the road,
When I jump in my car.

In my heart you'll always stay,
Until the very end . . .
My wonderful,
      Unbiased,
      Everlasting
      Truest *friend*!

Shehla Aslam

REGRETS

Darling, why did you leave me
I wanted to be the first to go.
You know I can't cope without you,
I've always loved you so.

We were boy and girl together
We grew up in the nicest way.
We always knew we would marry
At the church on the hill one day.

You left me here all alone.
I can't face the world without you
Why did you go? Honest I don't know
We were so happy we too.

But one day we'll be together
Once more we'll have a date.
I'm sure you'll be there smiling
To welcome me in Heaven's Gate.

Marjorie Wagg

ABSENT FRIEND

How I loved you long ago,
When I was an innocent child,
Your mane of dark brown hair,
Those big brown Irish eyes,
Which taught me to respect and be kind.

Hair then turned grey,
Smile on wrinkled face,
Eyes still bright as any summer morn,
You told me how you loved me and always will,
Though distance often kept us apart.

Then one lovely summer day,
Suddenly you passed away,
Never said goodbye to me.
Oh absent and best friend ever.
Mother dear you will live in my heart forever.

As Auld Lang Syne is sung with vigour,
Each New Year's Eve,
True memories live forever.

Kathleen Gosling

FAITHFUL FRIEND

Sprightly lightly
Flew our Collie in days gone by,
A streak of honey, such life.

The years pass and then
I ask of her once again
'Come sprightly lightly'

But now she's old still gold
      A special gem.
My girl her tail a waving feather,
With friendly heart her walk
      is talk of love for others
My friendly Collie,
      her paws patter slowly,
           along the pavement,
A heart of sage she
Follows brave with aged heart,
      hauling weight of time
           and years gone by.

She follows with faithful beat
      Old grace steady pace
         She sweet,
Her paws tap forwards, losing race
So I stop and wait
      for the friend of mine

Marian Freeman

PORTRAIT

I still see your hands,
your fingers taking their place,
touching softly on the faded ivory keys,
scribing your name upon my breast.

Your canvas in the bedroom,
soaked in colour and bliss,
the water frosting over,
passing the brush to me.

Whispering our songs
the melodic phrases,
those tones of spring,
I will never forget.

We are still together,
although time has taken you away,
I still hear you,
humming and whistling,
laughing with me.

I remember the day,
when you came to pass,
I smiled at the thought of you leaving,
being taken our of sight.

Separated on the outside,
but never within our hearts.

E W Griffiths

ANGEL IN A FRAME

I can see the light of love,
Shine out from eyes of blue,
I can see that sunny smile,
Reminding me of you,
I remember days gone by,
I'm still whispering your name
And I know I'll never lose you,
You're my angel in a frame,

You're my angel in a frame,
No-one can take away,
I can kiss you every morning,
I can hold you every day,
And when I'm sad and lonely,
I can set my heart aflame,
Just be looking at your picture,
You're my angel in a frame.

I can see you every morning,
And be with you every night,
I can talk to you each evening,
By the fires flickering light,
Though I know I can't be with you,
I'll love you just the same,
No-one can take you from me,
You're my angel in a frame.

Darrell Ryan

I HEAR A TINY HEARTBEAT

How precious now a single kiss
Upon your face
I often miss
Tender moments that we shared
You must have known
How much I cared

A yearning love that pains my heart
I feel such loss
We are apart
Yet you are oh so close to me
Within my soul
Inextricably

I hear a tiny heartbeat so
And every day
I feel it grow
Your gentle presence full of grace
I cherish now
Your smiling face

I pray dear Lord that you will keep
My precious Angel
Fast asleep
And kiss her sweetly every night
Caress her face
I wish I might

Karen E A Levick

UNTITLED

Where are the dreams that I once dreamed
Of happy days 'neath the sunny skies
Where everything would turn out right
In a world where friendship never dies

Where are the hopes that I held fast
Hopes of walking on through life
In true companionship and love
As we journeyed on as man and wife

Where are the plans that once I made
To do my best and win each game
To meet with fortitude and strength
The trials and the tests that came

Where are the thoughts that through my mind
Made every new day full of joy
Thoughts of all that could be done
If I would heart and mind employ

Where are the wishes that I wished
For health and wealth and happiness
For success in everything I did
For perfection . . . nothing less

Where are the friends that I have made
Those names which are so dear to me
Along with dreams and hopes and plans
They're safe within my memory.

Mary Whorlow

ALWAYS

My heart spills the tiny droplets
Caused by a wave, gigantic, thrashing waves
Of emotion, I feel for certain, you would not want me to sadden,
or feel alone.
But heart rules head at times, and I cannot help but ask why you were taken.
Every time I watch your favourite film, listen to your music,
Tread the now broken ground of your best loved places,
or taste your favourite foods, I feel you with me, never alone.
Our times together, too precious to lose.
Physically, no more can they happen, only memories are held by me.
Your laughter, tears, sadness and joy, the things you used to do,
or what you had to say, will happen no more, but are held always by me.
Something brought us together, in each other's lives, once our paths joined.
Now they are separated from our one.
The times we shared together from the very start, up until the time
you were called to go, I will always hold close.
They say time heals. What do they know?
Without you there, by my side.
You brought much into my life.
My friend, I miss you so very much.
Words cannot express my emotions, as they are so shattered,
so sprinkled, so difficult to mend.
Always, I feel you with me,
Encouraging and persuading me to keep on going,
enjoy life as it should be.
The one thing I cannot understand is, why so sudden, how come?
They have answers for everything, so they say.
But how, and why, cannot they answer my cries of pain, or give answers
to why you had to leave.
You told me no-one, and nothing, could separate us or stand in our way.
Your leaving does not change things.
I feel you with me, always.

Fiona Pearce

A FRIENDSHIP EVERLASTING

We have been good friends,
For so very long.
But they you said you had to go away,
What have I done wrong?

We've had our misunderstandings,
Like all close friends do,
But remembering the *good old days*,
Always helped us through.

They're taking you elsewhere,
Over the deep blue sea,
They don't seem to care
That they're taking you away from me.

Instead of seeing you every day,
Sharing a laugh and the odd moan,
We'll have to write what we want to say,
Or speak to each other down the phone.

When you've gone,
What will I do?
I'll just have to mope around,
And think about how much I miss you.

My parents say I'll make new friends,
They say life goes on still
But when I'm old and I have grey hair,
I'll think of you, I know I will.

You were my very best friend,
But now you've gone away,
You know I'll think of you all the time,
And in my heart you'll stay.

Dawn Oliver

STILL (FOR BETSY)

You were there
and I was somewhere else . . .
your arrival
evoked a scream of life
knife-edged, sharp and shrill
as I lay still
willing the nightmare to end

Your dream has just begun
fun-days
kisses, meadows, sky . . .

and I will hold you
as somehow
fate allowed us
to emerge together
whether or not our journeys
were the same
rain will still touch our faces
fine lace will still please our eyes
blue skies will still brighten our days

Your ways will still remind me
of my infant years
and your salt tears
will mix with mine
closing the fine line between us . . .
because
        although you were there
        and
I was somewhere else
you now recognise my smile
while you lie in my arms

heartbeat touching heartbeat
meeting together
a forever bond

Maroushka Monro

FRIENDS!

We share those special moments
That no-one else can see,
We often look at each other
Remembering times that we were free.
It's not that I don't see you
Your face, that loving smile,
But somehow it is different
We've know each other for a while.
Through our childhood years
We'd play silly games
Those long, hot summers
We're all the same.
The years have gone on
We've grown together,
I love you more now
We'll stay friends for ever.
Thank you my friend
For being there for me,
I hope for many more years
My best friend you will be.

Alanna Allen

THINKING OF YOU

My mind is filled with thoughts of you, and the pleasures that we shared.
Those special moments our friendship held, for two people who really cared.

It's little things that spring to mind, that bring sorrow to my heart,
My vision blurs with tears of sadness, from a friendship torn apart.

Friendship such as we had, was a once in a lifetime gift.
The cruel cruel blow that robbed me of you, came suddenly and swift.

I now must live from day to day with only the thoughts of you,
Longing to see you, touch you, smell you is now impossible to do.

Our friendship grew and bonded, as no other I have known.
I can't bear the thought I've lost you now, and feel sad and so alone.

If only you had told me of your illness, my dear friend,
I could have shared your fears of death, and been with you till the end.

I feel one day we will meet again, when it's my turn to face death.
But until that day you'll be in my thoughts, until my one last breath.

Brian Magee

FOR MARY

Buried our heads in upsurging grass
contented we'd be to let the hours pass
but for the clanging loud of the junior bell
that cast our dreams and broke the spell
of all our childish confidences
with each other - no pretences.
Met at eight we found the bond
and tied it tight and flung it far beyond
the school gate; sharing the joys
of every art; talk of the adolescent boys
with natural progression to our life adult
leading us to every dancing-favoured cult
and many a heartbreak sad romance
met in the glittering ballroom dance;
letters pounded back and forth when we parted were
in war, in peace, in gladness and in torment's blur;
and this our loyalty a lifetime's stood
and nothing now or ever will or could
our friendship break
and only death will separate.

Pamela Broster

FRIENDS FOR ALL OF TIME

The sun shines brightly
Shimmering and sparkling
on the sea
Where once it shone warmly
Upon you and me
We are there still I know
In the water in the sand
Friends holding hands

In the cold stark days
The snow glistens
in the trees
Where once it fell coldly
Upon you and me
We are there still I know
In the cold in the dark
Friends holding hands

A tear drops softly
in the silent dark
Where once it never fell
And we were apart yet
We are there still I know
In the sun in the moon
In the light in the dark
Friends holding hands

Patricia Willis Taylor

THE PHOTOGRAPH

'How long ago did first we meet?
At toddler class when with stamping feet
You showed your disdain of the music sweet
By stomping away to your mum?'

'Oh no,' eyes drop with a winsome smile,
''twas when our prams came to rest awhile,
Your gran looked into my pram and said:
'What a puny child! Look at mine instead!
She's a perfect picture of health!'

You were the rebel and I was so good,
Small wonder, indeed, we fell out and stood
On opposite sides of the friendship tree.
I thought, 'How could she do this to me?'
Take her down a peg!' You thought.

As years went by you mellowed - and I?
Now I was the rebel. To hue and cry
And protest marches I did fly.
You sat and listened to all my tales
And smiled your winsome smile.

So, fifty years on, we are still around
And our edges are smoother where time has ground.
Now our daughters, too, are in friendship bound.
Common interests they have found.
Will they stand the test of time?

And here we are on your garden seat
Where all the years that are past now meet.
The camera clicks. The smiles are sweet
In a photo which makes the tale complete
On a sunny afternoon.

Rosemary Lane

ON EARTH AS IT IS IN HEAVEN (A DEBATE)

Physicists in the business of feeling for infinity
May freely agree they see God.
Now Jesus' beliefs and his books about divinity
Are reopened to them which seems odd.

Microscopes and telescopes,
Elaborate apples of Eve,
Electronic, hypnotic to raise strange hopes,
Believe or be deceived?

'My friends, do you reckon there ever is He,
Or could be or was or will ever be as truth?
'Not too clever,' I protest, 'dim Biblical simplicity.
Look deep, look elsewhere. Stuff this spoof!'

Telescopes and microscopes,
Eternally search for the infinite,
For Alpha outside and Omega in they grope,
Until logic develops a test for it?

'But what is not matter, matters much more,'
They turn on me to explain.
'It matters more even than matter itself,' they bore
With blind certainty, saying, 'See, He comes again!'

For Christ is our friend who is also in space,
On His way, He's the Word, the creator and gate.
He's intricate and infinite: everywhere His face.
He's the light we are looking by: Jesus, our mate.

Kenneth Lane

CRY TEARS

Cry tears now we've lost the chance
to partner you in life's fine dance,
you gave in, you got what you want
and left the pain with us.

We tried to give importance to
impress the gift they gave to you
and maybe we could push you through
the pain you left with us.

And though you thought that life's not fair
the people here have tried to care,
but all you did was sit and stare
at the pain you left with us.

The reasons why you find yourself
so all alone, in need of help
are lost to us, although we've felt
the pain you left with us.

So consider the subtle irony
of the life you could have had with me
it's good to share, why can't you see
the pain you left with us.

But you gave in at the very start
and leant against your broken heart,
you didn't even want a part
of the pain you left with us.

So cry tears now we've lost the fight
to pull you through and keep it tight
and all we've got to offer tonight
is the pain you left with us.

Derek Reeves

PROUD TO CALL YOU FRIEND

The whole world seems against you, you feel so sad and blue,
Nothing seems to go right, you want to start anew.
The plans that once you dreamed of have all come to an end,
But there's still someone beside you, proud to call you friend.

Winter storms are with you, spring is far away,
Days are cold and dreary, skies are always grey.
There seems no joy or gladness, will it never end?
He's waiting there to cheer you, proud to call you friend.

The dark clouds are above you, they never seem to break.
No-one seems to love you, it is more than you can take.
The folk who once you trusted, on whom you could depend,
There is still one close beside you, proud to call you friend.

You have had your share of trouble, he knows that well enough,
Sorrow, care and heartache, the going has been tough.
But you know you are not forgotten, broken hearts will mend,
He'll be there right beside you, proud to call you friend.

A shoulder for you to cry on, comfort that you seek
He is always there to listen to every word you speak.
Two gentle arms to hold you, his are yours to lend
He's standing right beside you, proud to call you friend.

He does not ask for favours, he is just sincere and true,
He wants to give you courage, to see you smiling through,
When the going gets harder, you can't see round the bend,
He is still there right beside you, proud to call you friend.

Now the skies are brighter, sunshine follows rain,
Your heart seems so much lighter, you start to smile again,
Just take a look around you, you knew you could depend,
On the one you see beside you, proud to call you friend.

B Luffman

A SHOULDER TO CRY ON

Come to me my dearest friend
My arms are open wide
My door is always open
Come and step inside.

My shoulder awaits your tears
Your sadness to unfold
I know you have a troubled mind
Come in out of the cold

The fire is lit, the kettle on,
No need to fight the tears.
Sit right here and tell me all that's wrong,
We've been friends for many years.

It doesn't matter, I've got the time
Just let is all come out.
What has happened to make you sad?
What is it all about?

We talk, we cry, we try to smile
But the time is getting on.
It doesn't matter how long it takes
Jobs can be done when you've gone..

To share your troubles halves your troubles
And now you're not so sad
Bye bye to you my dearest friend
Things don't seem quite so bad.

Valerie Hall

AUTOMATIC

I naturally cling to you,
like a babe to its mother's bosom.
I naturally cling to you,
for the friend in you,
for the friend that was, and still is, in you.
It's automatic, sometimes sweeter, sometimes tragic.

I naturally cling to you,
because of the natural love in you
I naturally cling to you and instantaneously like
the labour pains of female body,
it's automatic.
I naturally cling to you and a catalysis occurred.
Automatic, sometimes sweeter, sometimes tragic.

And like a lover holds its lover's hand,
And like when mother talks and child understands
I naturally cling to the words of you,
simply because they involve you.
It simply would be non-automatic not to
cling to the being of you.

Natalie George

YOU AND ME

We've always been together,
Jived through our teens together
In stockings with seams together,
And with every year
You were always near.

Brought up our kids together,
Counted our quids together,
Borrowed pan lids together,
And when I'd need you
You'd always come through.

Now we are old together,
We feel the cold together,
Our friendship's such
That I hope very much
That we'll be interred together.

Sheila G Farrow

A THANK YOU POEM TO MY BEST FRIENDS

Mum and Dad, I know you're glad
For all the joyous years you had
Now I wish to thank you both
My life, you gave, I give on oath
These eyes to see, the beauty that's surrounding me
Flowers, trees, the earth, the sky
I'll feast on these before I die.
Meadows green to walk upon
Legs supporting all day long
Creative hands that I may paint
From photographs, though out of date
In bygone days, I'd rather be
Happy times, just you and me
Songs and tunes from yesteryear
Without my ears I could not hear
A nose that's large and somewhat rare,
Equipped to sniff the country air
Two strong arms that embrace
Loved ones, whom my favours grace
And for my heart that I may love
Those on earth, and those above
Although I often shed a tear
Somehow I know that you are near.

Maureen Weitman

THE GARDEN GATE

I was a soldier's lonely wife,
You were beginning married life
We shared our sadness
Happiness and joy,
We both gave birth
To a baby boy.
We shared coffee, cups of tea
Ate a bun, when we were hungry.
Now so many miles apart
We keep in touch by letters and phone.
It's wonderful knowing a person who cares,
Treasures our friendship
In so many ways.
It all started long ago
Was it luck, or really fate
The night we met
Near a garden gate.

Hilda Mawer

A DEAR PERSON

This man is the father of my child,
One minute angry but soon he is mild.
We have our sorrow, tears and gladness,
Not many hours are spent in sadness.
We quarrel, oh yes, and disagree,
But this man means the world to me.

He entered my life many years ago,
But still I am learning about him now.
On major decisions we see eye to eye,
To him I would find it hard to lie.
As time goes on we will help each other,
This husband of mine, my only lover.

M Goodwin

FOREVER FRIENDS

I recall I was 12 when we met
At first we hurled abuse over the garden fence . . . and yet
Beyond growing pains, adolescence and puberty our friendship stood
Through teenage years to womanhood
Later her bridesmaid I became, then godmother to her only son
How I cried when she left, with her husband and my godson aged one

A fresh start in New Zealand, so far away
I'll never forget saying goodbye that day
Convinced we'd never meet again
Fifteen years of friendship down the drain

I missed our Friday nights, sharing hopes and dreams
Worries and heartaches, plans and schemes
No more words of comfort after an ended love affair
No-one to turn to, a secret to share

Letters, tapes, photos, cards, an occasional fleeting visit back here
Other friendships grew but none so dear

After many years she's come back home to stay
Returning to England and her family too
She's residing in Norfolk, still miles away
But one Friday night soon we'll sit together and reminisce as old friends do
We'll recall the dances and fancy dress balls, when we dressed in
                                             ridiculous gear
The hamster we shared, can't remember its name but those days remain
                                             vivid and clear
So having cast our minds back, with all thoughts exchanged
We'll turn to each other and agree nothing has changed

Angela Edwards

ABSENT FRIENDS

The little girl across the way
I went to school with every day.
Then after school we used to play,
She's always in my memory.
Then came the parting of the way,
Though we are still in touch today.
Then came the time my life was gay,
I used to dance the night away.
I'd many friends I soon forgot,
Though some I care for quite a lot.
There also was a special three,
Who always have remembered me.
Then I got married settled down,
Bought a little house near town,
My next door neighbours they were grand,
They always gave a helping hand.
Now they are living far away,
Yet I still hear from them today.
I've also friends across the sea
Who never have forgotten me.
So as I make a toast today
To absent friends who are away
My thoughts will all go back in time
As I am singing Auld Lang Syne.

Clarice Rothwell

MY DEAREST MUM

I close my eyes and see her there before me,
Arms outstretched and smiling ever sweetly.
She who knew my innermost emotions,
In whom I could confide and trust completely.

Nine years have passed since last we were together.
I held her loving hand until the end
And whispered humble thanks for all her caring,
Then she was gone - dear Mum - my lifelong friend.

I still can hear her ever-present laughter.
Her warmth shines on though we must be apart,
Inspiring me to treasure all life's beauty,
An absent friend forever in my heart.

Jean Christie

ANNETTE

'I wonder who will be my friend?'
That is what you said your first morning at school,
As we stood by the gate at the road end.
In the playground, children, unheeding,
Ran, tumbled, walked, skipped, danced.
Talked, shouted, shrieked, laughed, cried.
Everywhere, movement and noise.
Crowding, thinning, ebbing, flowing all around.
A bewilderment of children.

Were you frightened, overwhelmed by the strangeness?
You shed no tears.
There were no tantrums or hysterics.
But your handclasp tightened as you said
'I wonder who will be my friend?'
She found you that day; your friend.
Out of the playground hubbub and frenzy
She came - Annette.
First friend, good friend, firm friend.
Now far away, but not forgotten.

D M Dudley

ODE TO AN ABSENT FRIEND

When I first set my eyes on you
    I knew right from the start
That fate had meant you to be mine
    'Twas then you stole my heart.

Who could resist that glossy coat
    Those dangling ears, those eyes,
That could be so mischievous
    and other times, so wise?

The hours and hours we walked along
    The shady lanes, together,
Across the fields, along the beach
    in every kind of weather.

You were my dear companion
    You knew when I felt ill
You seemed to understand my mood
    I know you always will.

You were a source of laughter, too
    So full of fun, always.
A playful, yet obedient, friend
    You filled my lonely days.

I really thought my heart would break
    The sad day you left me.
I buried you in the garden
    that's where you'd want to be.

Who can know the sorrow of
    the loss of a loving pet?
His love for me, his faithfulness
    I never can forget.

O J Adams

FRIENDS FOREVER

It's over a year
Since I saw you last,
But I've not let you fade,
Into memories of my past.
You're my oldest friend,
But with every letter,
I learn something new.
Get to know you better.

I know you're still there
When I feel alone,
When I'm upset or afraid,
I just pick up the phone;
And you cheer me up,
With stories that we told
Of our fairy tale prince,
When we were not very old.

I know we'll be friends
For the rest of forever.
I will see you soon,
When we've time to get together.
We'll remember old times,
Share our memories of the past;
You were my friend first,
And I'll have your friendship last.

Tara L Huddless

ALWAYS FRIENDS

Where are you! Where are you!
You're always there when I need you
But now the first doubt
A missing space like a gap in time
Have I taken you for granted?
Have I assumed too much?
I am just not sure
Where should I look, what should I do
In times of crisis you have always been there

Time passes in chunks of moments
Sometimes quick but often slow
Perception of ten minutes is nearer three hours
Just when panic was on the verge
There was a calm, an assurance, a voice

Hello my love, I am here
I know I have been away
I know we have parted by distance
Though not through feelings and thought
We have not been as one together in matrimony
But there is a bonding, a closeness, a friendship
So many years, so many memories
They will not fade or disappear nor do I wish it
We may go our separate ways with blessing on each other
But the tie, the communications, the understanding will live
As friends we are now, we shall always be.

Philip M Smith

DO YOU REMEMBER?

Do you remember, my old pal,
the day that we first met.

It was our first day at school,
we both felt scared and sick.

We grew together through the years,
sitting side by side.

Or playing rugby for the school,
remember when you broke your leg.

We went to dances, dated girls,
and had a drink or three.

As times passed by, we both got wed,
then we had our kids.

But sadly things went wrong for both of us,
divorce is not a pretty word.

But we stood together through the storm,
remained the best of friends.

We've had our ups and downs since then,
And I don't see you so much.

But though thirty years and more have passed,
I know that if I am in a scrape

Then you will be there for me my friend,
no matter where you are.

R J Curry

VANESSA

I didn't know in '82 when our mums met that day
That fourteen years would pass, and our friendship would stay
And as I look back, a smile appears
Like the one on your face, when we've talked through our fears.

Do you remember the school trips we shared?
And the phone calls which showed me that you really cared.
Our first days at school were a little scary,
But together we discovered there was no need to be wary.

I've helped you survive a Guide Camp, and more,
And you've always listened, even though I can bore.
I'm glad you were there when we got lost down that lane,
I know I won't make that mistake again.

OK, we've disagreed on things, but they're in the past
They were silly irritations which didn't last.
I hope when I have children they will see
That having a good friend will make them as lucky as me.

Soon, we'll be separated when university arrives,
But I'm sure we'll stay friends for the rest of our lives.
I know you'll stand by me whatever I do
It's important for me to say thank you to you.

Laura Charleton (17)

REUNION

The train arrived, she scanned the crowded platform
To glimpse again at last the face so dear
The one who was the kindest and most caring
Her absence felt through every passing year

They'd shared their youthful secrets and their wishes
Amongst the pots and pans of houses grand
Until the day had come when one had married
And travelled to a far too distant land

Through all of twenty years their parting lasting
Though letters helped to keep the two in touch
And now at last the long-awaited meeting
The day that she had thought about so much

Feelings came to her of doubt and apprehension
So long parted could she find the words to say
Then through the crowds there came the dear-loved figure
As though her friend had never been away

Sylvia Hillman

OVER THIRTY YEARS

Our friendship started man years ago
How it ever lasted, I will never know.
At first it was a clash of wills,
The path was long and all up hills.
This love was spiritual and good,
If anything it understood
That only if it was the best
Could this friendship pass the test.
His partner gone now, and the tears
What held the lonely future years?
His body was tired and terminally ill,
Life gave him duties to fulfil.
We met again, both being free,
There was no future we could see,
But love that gives demands no prize,
For it is written in the skies.
Heaven is just a peaceful state
To sit, to talk, to meditate.
We helped each other through this veil
He's waiting for me, I can tell.
Our friendship overcame the gloom,
We'll meet again, it will resume.

B M Bryan

GOODBYE AUNT ROSE

My dear Aunt Rose,
You sit alone and nod in quiet repose,
And who can tell
What thoughts possess the aunt I knew so well.
You were my guide;
When I was young and needed to confide
In someone who
Would understand, I always came to you.

I watch you now . . .
You didn't always have that wrinkled brow,
Nor hair so grey
Where once a golden halo softly lay.
Once in a while
Far memories evoke a secret smile . . .
In misty eyes
A lifetime's joys and sorrows harmonise.

Your summer's gone
But oh, my fading Rose, you linger on
And break my heart,
Because as strangers we must surely part;
You don't know me
Now you have slipped into senility,
But fear no pain . . .
In heaven's garden you shall bloom again.

Wendy Fry

FRIENDS

Forget me not, dear companion
I have often come this way and thought 'How time stands still . . . '
And yet it's not the sound of your voice
Or your cheery smile that make me think of you
It's the murmuring hum of the factory, the smell of smoking chimneys
And the way you used to knot your tie.
I wonder how you think of me,
I'm sure you must.
Because we have shared so much of life's rich weave
And though we may now seldom meet, because our lives tread
                                              different paths,
You are as much a part of me as I,
The games we played as clear as yesterday
And if you should chance upon those same grey streets
Don't mourn the past or rue the day we left.
It's all still there as vibrant as it was
And neither time, nor separation, can change a love like that
What we had then is here and now, and always.

Derek Charles Fuller

FOR MIDGE

The meaning of 'Life' is found in a friend,
It is found in your heart, and the hand you extend.

It can be rippling laughter or the depths of despair,
It can be without reason, but your friends are still there.

It emanates earthwards from God's gracious love,
And continues hereafter in heaven above.

We will hold you so gently in your moments of strife,
As we grow all together in the meaning of life.

Doreen Britton

YOU AND ME

I always see us as we used to be,
Two children playing games and running wild,
And oh! What fun it was to be a child,
Unfettered, happy, smiling friends were we
Without a care, our hearts and minds were free,
And people seeing us together smiled,
And by our mutual love they were beguiled,
But did not really know the you and me.
If ever I was mournful, feeling sad,
You'd comfort me and make me feel at ease,
A twinkle in your eye could make me glad
And vanish sadness, tears and sobs appease.

And tho' you have been gone these thirty years,
You yet can make me laugh and calm my fears.

Maggie Cardew

PALS

We'd been pals for many years,
Sharing joys and hopes and tears.
Always ready with word or deed
And there to listen when in need.
Never a quarrel as time went by,
Telling the truth refusing to lie.
Giving each other a lift when we were down,
Facing our troubles with a grin not a frown.
Standing shoulder to shoulder when crisis loomed,
Giving three rousing cheers when success bloomed.
Always supportive whether sick or healthy,
No complaints because we'd never be wealthy.
We always enjoyed laughter, refused the tears,
That's why we stayed married for so many years.

Ted Rolls

STILL FRIENDS

With confident air
With auburn hair
Friends from the start
Sincere at heart
Freckled of face
I'll never erase
Complexion clean, peaches and cream
Welsh she spoke and
hand in hand
A special bond
Had a ball, sharing all
Tidy and neat the world to meet
Edith Bach
Navy blue and white tie just right
Polished shoes and black
stockinged legs
A special time our hearts entwined
Step out together taking care
Having words, there we were
Spending youth
Smiles and tear
those two years
On the Mull, never dull
Dear to my heart
Edith Bach
As chalk and cheese
we tried to please
Told me off, never strayed
from womanly ways
Keep in touch, remembering when
you were a Wren.
My other half, Edith Bach.

Connie Moseley

COMRADESHIP

I found it as a young man, a naval rating SBA
On board a fighting ship out the Pacific way
Comradeships then, left grief when parting made
Just like leaving one's family, from sunlight to shade
But only a moment, our lives full as adventure sought
Wondering if fortune beckoned us, what port
Would welcome with open arms, what charms
Indeed what other challenges we'd meet
One found this awaiting us with the Pacific fleet
It's found in adversity, we all need each other
Far from home, each needing an adopted brother
Young men, independent of mothers' apron strings
Have to suddenly grow up, really spread their wings
Us naval chaps we had oppos' slang for pal or mate
Blood brothers scarcely apart unless a special date
I didn't really have an oppo though plenty to call pal
Going off on my own at times, never with another gal
I wrote home to one lass and kept faith with her
Right until the day I came home from the war
Soon after that friendship abated, for a while felt deflated
Though had many friendships since, some just in passing
Some that have and will continue to last a lifetime
To remain the very essence of good comradeship.

P Temperton

FRIENDS

Don't turn your back and walk away,
Please stay until the end,
I need someone to call a friend,
My life is upside-down right now,
I don't know what to do,
Please be my friend, don't walk away,
That's all I ask of you.

Some things that I have said,
have hurt you just as much,
Please be my friend and hold my hand,
I need to feel your touch,
There are not many people,
I can really call my friend,
One day you'll need me just as much,
And I'll stay until the end.

Joanne Aisthorpe

YOU AND I

In thoughts of you I spend my days
Just willing you to phone
We shared so much in many ways
Just you and I alone.

We talked for hours, I loved each minute
My senses overthrown
I had no life 'til you were in it
Just you and I alone.

We shared our hopes, our dreams, our fears
I realised love had grown
The days made weeks, the weeks made years
Just you and I alone.

You come and go, and I still care
As you have always known
I wish that we were still back there
Just you and I alone.

It's years since you first said goodbye
The world you had to roam
So now I write, with tear in eye
For you . . . and I alone.

G D Wakefield

FRIENDS FOREVER

We've been together through the years
My trusting friend and I.
We loved each other from the start
And never wondered why.
We danced with joy when things were right,
We cried when things were wrong,
The friendship blossomed day by day,
Brought to our hearts a song.
We laughed and played throughout the years
When life was good and sweet,
Then came the time when things were bad,
Life crumbled round our feet.
When bombs rained down around our home
We hugged each other tight,
We clung together through dark hours
Until the morning light.
Throughout life's troubles, joys and fears,
We wandered hand in hand,
And now, as time is growing short,
Together still we stand.
Whenever I am feeling sad,
We share the same armchair;
He comforts me, he gives me hope,
My darling teddy bear.

Margaret Collins

FRIENDSHIP

Time has no span, nor age its limitation.
A sun kissed garden
Of memories of warmth, and of frustration.
Of flowers which die.
And youth which is forsaken.

Time has not changed, the sea of life
Has ebbed and flowed again.
A friendship undisturbed by years
As autumn leaves, or summer flowers unfold,
We meet again.

Time, as old or young as human heart desires
Is forever, and for now.
A life, a death, it matters not.
Faith keeps within my soul
A memory.

Helen Towner

UNTITLED

For you are the sister of my heart and soul.
As a child you were my playmate,
As a teenager you were my friend,
As a woman you are my most precious companion.
Through time, life has challenged us both.
Time and distance played as rivalries against us.
All I am, you have seen.
All sides of my soul, both black and white.
Never once have you turned your back upon me.
Through embraced arms we have wept.
Through held hands we have run through cornfields,
With the sound of laughter ringing through our ears.
All that you are, I have always wanted to be,
For you are the strong one,
The beautiful one,
The kind and generous one.
For you the sun shall always shine on.
Oh friend of mine . . .

Anne-Marie Rose

FRIENDSHIP

Friendships old, friendships new,
Yet nothing stirs the memory like old friends do.
That unsettling moment when the past is with you,
Brought to the present by the playing
Of some old tune remembered.
Or while idling the time away you find yourself
Suddenly smiling and you have to laugh aloud,
When all else around you are wondering why.
Treasured memories shared by two,
When one is absent tend to make one sigh,
Reminiscing of things gone by
Is it that the past is so rosy and
That I'm missing a friend so true,
Or is it a feeling of what might have
Been, now that my life's two thirds through.
Thoughts of what could have been
Instead of how they are,
Tend to make you blue,
Thoughts of escaping the status quo,
Of two companions alike in thought and deed,
Unfettered and carefree enjoying
Life and full of glee.
Oh where are you now my friend,
Why did our friendship ever have to end?

Peter Ley

A MEMORY OF A FRIEND

There was once a friend
And she was indeed
A friend in need
When she helped me with my child

She helped me after my pregnancy
She helped me to oversee
All chores and gave me
Endless cups of tea

I am afraid
That she has now passed
But the memory of my friend
Will remain in my mind

Luciene Azique

TO AN ABSENT FRIEND

I forgot my old school friend,
for many fast moving years.
We had shared our hopes and fears,
there were intimate letters penned.
We were reunited recently
and vowed to see each other frequently.
We met at a restaurant in Islington,
where with old classmates,
we shared a lunch date.
Our visit to Cambridge city
was one of history and beauty,
ending with a punt on the river.
I remember the pleasant picnics
by Grafham and Rutland Water
in the summer idyllic.
The dynamic interaction
was present as of yesteryear.
It took no imagination
to time travel and to hear
voice speaking from school days.
We wish we lived nearer each other,
experiences to unite always.
Will we meet often in the future?

Heather Horlock

ME AND PETE

I remember, of course I do,
When we were boys in fifty two,

We played cricket, not too well
And football in seasons in Maddox Dell,

Made bow from yew, firing golden rod,
And walked the downs on Fetcham's Sod.

Cut long sticks from the hazel groves
Just like *Little John*
Climbed old oak trees, with the help
Of a rope, how long gone.

We waited for snow to silence the
Sounds of partridge and dove,
Sledding from light until dark,
Cold fingers, wet trousers, wet stockings and glove.

At Christmas, we went from your house to mine,
Comparing gifts and cheeking our mums,
Catching our dads at the scotch
And us on wine gums.

So long ago, quite another age,
If it was world history, not even a page.

But a chapter recorded in our lifetime, friend,
As we get much nearer to our history's end.

Anthony John

PATRICIA

Nine months together, sharing the warmth,
The beat of our mother's heart.

I lived, but I hadn't shared, I hadn't cared.
I didn't even say Goodbye.
Too late, I tried to share, divide my dinners.
Too late, I tried to care. Feed her. Feed her!
Was it caring? Sharing? Instinct?
Some infantile gesture of repentance?
Too late, those dreams of embrace,
Of that closeness in the dark warmth.
Oh the guilt of all those years.

But now, led by the Spirit, back,
Back to the spring of our birth;
Repentance!
Not a gesture this time,
But real, tear flowing, heart sobbing, earth kneeling repentance!
I starved my sister, my own dear sister;
Kicked her to survive.
I am sorry, dear Patricia, so, so sorry.

I am forgiven, she has forgiven me.
We didn't say Goodbye,
For we will once more embrace,
Patricia and I,
And share the beat of our mother's heart.
How the angels will celebrate that reunion
In the womb of Heaven.

John Hampson

POT OF GOLD

When we were married, sixty years ago,
We set up house in a terraced row.
Soon we became friends with the couple next door,
Never dreaming our friendship would last evermore.
We sailed through calm waters, conquered stormy weather,
Our children played and grew up together.
We were so happy, then came the war,
With our men at the front, it bound us more.
At last peace was declared, the fighting was over,
With our men safely home, we were once more in clover.
The years passed by until one day
Our friend's husband, he passed away.
Now for sixty years she has been our friend,
A friend on whom we can depend.
If you find such a friend, young or old,
You will have found yourself *a pot of gold*.

Hilda Naughton

UNTITLED

We talked, we smiled, we laughed together
The day we two first met.
From that moment it was meant to be
The pattern somehow set.
We've shared so much throughout the years
Happiness, secrets, sometimes tears.
As life goes on and we grow old
Silver threads amongst the gold.
A bond we two have formed together
A bond, we know will last forever.
Whatever happens, always depend
On a true and loyal, loving friend.

Bridget Ward

DISTANCE AND DISCOS

My tears, as I spoke, made the receiver wet,
As she listened to me speak of why my dog was with the vet.

Ten minutes later I cried with laughter as she spoke about
A guy from college she can clearly *do without.*

Only a week later, clubbily clad,
We're staggering to the Ritzy, after that lad.

The streets were silent and icy and our taxi for the wrong destination,
We curled up at the foot of the phone box in deep conversation . . .

For the three years previous, I feel we grew apart
Though she was in my heart for the most part.

Over that time I've moved away and the distance now more,
our homes and lives had blended into one before.

You don't really think much about it but ambition tears you away,
I'm studying clothing design and she's studying for a stage play.

Sometimes now communication is only a phone call or letter,
But our friendship's far stronger than when I'd just met her.

We recall my eighteenth birthday when we went out for a meal,
And a cold breezy night in fun company on a Ferris wheel.

I thought that distance had changed everything
But when I need to talk I'll pick up the phone and give her a ring.

It's not any less important to us, just different ,you see,
Your friends are behind you - you've got to grab opportunity.

Samantha Bate

FRIENDSHIP BLUES

Standing on the corner
Don't know which way to choose,
  Shaking hands, sometimes I find,
  Brings on the friendship blues.

All my life packed in a bag,
I hear that whistle call,
  Don't need you here at my side,
   No, don't need you here at all.

I heard them sing in different time,
They said I'd never lose,
  But, being put down by a friend
  Just brings on the friendship blues.

They've helped me with their outstretched hands,
They've also seen me fall.
  But no-one ever helped me up,
   No, not as I recall.

So now I travel with my mind,
 No-one to lose my way.
  Drifting's faster by yourself,
  And keeps the blues away.

Terry Bobrowicz

UNTITLED

We met when we were barely five
We started school together
Now over half a century on
There's nothing we can't weather

We shared some tears and lots of joys
We even shared some of the boys
If one of us didn't have a date
The other one's boyfriend would bring a mate

We both were wed in '61
She's had two children, I had none
I loved her kids like they were mine
Now she's a grandma and that's just fine.

Although I moved to the Isle of Wight
We meet when we are able
I never want to lost contact
With my very best friend *Mabel*.

Carol A Maddison

A FRIEND

I had a friend today,
We talked
We shared
Our souls were bared.
I had a friend today,
We planned
We laughed
We evolved
Our thoughts were resolved.
I had a friend today,
We delved
We revealed
Loneliness was healed.
I had a friend today,
We agreed
We discussed
Our minds did trust.
I have a friend,

Today.

Pauline Jones

FRIENDS AND LOVERS

I seem to have a problem here
to which the answer isn't clear.
They really don't like one another,
my best friend and latest lover.

He's only known her for a week,
He says,
'She's got a bloody cheek to turn up
here in floods of tears. You haven't seen
the girl for years!'

OK, it's true. He has a case,
but God it's good to see her face and listen
to her silly chatter.
Do time and distance really matter?

She says,
'I think the guy's a fool. It's obvious
he wants to rule the way that you should
lead your life. He's looking for another wife!'

Time has proved that she was right.
I threw him out after a fight.
She'll laugh when she receives my letter signed
'You win - I can do better!'

Loraine Darcy

MY ABSENT FRIEND

My absent friend is Shaza,
I saw her every day.
We were best friends together,
perfect in every way.

But then we had to go
into separate schools.
So then my life was over,
my life now had no rules.

We write letters to each other,
in most of our spare time.
I tell all my problems to her,
in more than just one line.

We will always be friends,
for ever and ever.
One of a kind
like birds of a feather.

Laura Parkinson (11)

KEEPING IN TOUCH
(To an absent friend)

Although you're thousand of miles away
I'll send you letters come what may,
They'll remind you of years gone by
When we were together you and I.
I'll tell you of the good things
Of what joy to my life brings.
Remind you of jokes we shared
How for each other we always cared.
Although you're thousands of miles away
I'll never forget your special day,
When you became a happy bride,
How I admired you with pride,
Our childhood days are long ago
But a photograph or two will show -
Our smiling faces revealing pleasure,
Past times I will always treasure.
At school we had such sport and fun,
More than once a prize you won.
Oh, absent friend we'll meet again
As in a dream down memory lane.

F Norris

TO FRIENDSHIP

It's a happy man who has a friend,
Someone on whom he can rely,
For all things in this modern world,
Wealth cannot true friendship buy,
A friend who's solid shoulder's there,
Each time you need to cry,
Who sees you through each crisis,
Without ever asking why,
A friend who's joy is your joy,
And who's love for you is real,
Who listens to your troubles,
And knows exactly how you feel.

For when that friend has gone away,
To a place you cannot follow,
At first there seems to be a space,
What was solid, now seems hollow,
But soon that space is filled again,
With memories so demanding,
Of happy times, of love, and joy,
And quiet understanding.,
Like pictures, each in silver frames,
Our mind's eyes still retaining,
For though the friend's no longer there,
The friendship's still remaining.

Ann Williams

LASTING FRIENDSHIP

We were both seventeen when first we met, on a cold December day
as we waited for a bus to come to take us on our way
Into the city we were going to work
she to office, I to shop
But what a lot has happened since that meeting at bus stop.

We travelled to and fro each day, and had a laugh with all the crew
Also the other travellers, and so out friendship grew.
For several years we did that journey,
Until at last I wed,
before moving to the city, and later children had.

She'd visit me from time to time and stay awhile for tea
She'd then play with my little lads
who'd giggle happily,
Then one day I got a letter saying 'she was getting wed,
and we were all invited 'we'd be pleased to come,' I said.

In her village church we gathered, to hear them pronounced man and wife
Then onto the little village hall,
where we wished them a happy life.
Shortly after getting married, they moved away up North
But our friendship still continued, with our letters back and forth.

Now she has children of her own, and like me grandchildren too
And still we regularly correspond,
sharing our points of view.
We're now both sixty five years old, so that's forty eight years since the day,
we met at that country bus stop on a cold December day.

*No doubt we'll meet again one day, but until the time we do
I'll look forward to the letters, from Joan, my friend so true.*

M Weavers

MY OLD TED

My old Ted, a friend quite true,
As years go by, and there's been a few.
When you were young your fur would shine.
I held you in small hands of mine.
But now you're older, yes - same as me
With worn out bits and parts to see.
Worn with cuddles through the years
You helped me get through all my fears.
You were there when I learned to walk
You listened mute as I learned to talk
And while the years went rolling by
You sat and watched with steady eye.
When teens approached still on my bed,
At night I'd touch you gentle head
You gave me comfort through and through
Without your help what would I do
When I married and became a wife
You came too! Part of my life.
And now you're cuddled by daughter small
You see, you're much loved by us all
Worn and ragged you might be
But you're still the best old friend to me.

F M Rapley

SOUL MATES

I love autumn skies he said to me
Visions of light and tranquillity.
Mantles of blue reach far out of sight
Bright twinkling stars that come out at night.
To be friends with him has meant so much
To walk by his side and feel his touch
An inner peace we share together
Oh let it go on for ever and ever.

We walk life's path on earth together meet people every day.
Some are meant to be good friends others fade away.
But the one who's become my special friend
I keep within my heart
This love contains no boundaries even when apart.
A friendship that is deep and true goes on and on forever
There's nothing in the whole wide world that it can ever sever.

June Mills

MY OLD ACQUAINTANCE

Should old acquaintance be forgot?
It sounds a good idea.
This climate here's lovely and hot
And airmail costs are dear.

My old acquaintance has forgot,
For I sent a card last year.
Don't know if he got it or not,
But he didn't return one here.

Perhaps old acquaintances are best forgot
It's so hard for me to see.
If he's still upset as I won a lot
On football coupon he paid for me.

An old acquaintance sadly forgot,
The taste of our old pub's beer.
That draught here, they haven't got,
So buying brewery to make it here.

Goodbye old acquaintance I haven't forgot,
From my winnings you're owed a share.
Enclose 50p refund, from my yacht,
My coupons cost you paid back there!

Martin Ford

THREADS OF GOLD

A friendship woven
The pictures unfold;
Streams of living waters
Resembling threads of gold.

At times you were an island,
Far, far away,
Caressed by timeless thoughts,
As your shores appeared grey.

Contrasting moments gathered
Across life's ocean spans.
Friendly souls in harmony,
Sharing hopes and plans.

Lingering dreams have manifest
Like sunbeams glowing.
Others fade away and die,
That's how life keeps flowing.

Sunlight always sifting
The golden threads,
While more subdued thoughts,
Our memory sheds.

Through all of life's journeys
And colourful days,
We draw together golden threads,
To catch the sun's rays.

Lesley Lyn

END OF AN ERA

Who can I turn to
Now that she's gone?
Who'll make me laugh
When the hours feel so long?
Who will chase away
The frown upon my face,
And when the sky is dull
Put sunshine in it's place?
How can I help
This desolate feeling,
When she is not here
To give life meaning?

D M Gibbons

PEN FRIENDS

We are pen friends who
Write from me to you
Keeping in touch
It means so much
Minds reaching out
As we talk about
Family goings on
And gardening done
Somehow we share
Our need and to care
About all sorts of things
Each writer brings
To the empty pages
Our hopes our joys our rages

Jenny Major

FRIENDSHIPS GAIN

You were six and I was five
When into my life you came;
We laughed and played, fought and made
A friendship strong, with love displayed
In childish innocence.

I wore a locket on my chain
Your face and mine within the frame;
Entwined together through the years
It seemed to me that life would be,
Impossible without you.

Time parted us too soon it seemed
To go our different ways;
We met, we kept in touch, by letter
and the trains that meant so much.
The distances they seemed so vast
A test to make our friendship last,
We knew it would.

Older now, yet friends we still remain,
the telephone has long ago replaced the train;
But it was you who sealed our fate
In friendships lasting gain;
For you did something beautiful,
You gave your child my name.

Carolyn R Byrom

A BELATED FRIEND

I'll always remember the friendship of a girl I knew at school,
We were like twins together, swimming in a pool.
Little secrets we would share, plenty of those we had,
We'd whisper all about the boys, who we thought we bad.
But one fatal day on the tennis court, alas my friend she died,
I couldn't seem to control myself, however hard I tried.
Now I'm older, I look back on the fun we had together,
When we played outside, in all kinds of weather.
Life goes on as well we know, I'll never forget my friend,
My heart was nearly broken, but now her grave I tend.

Chris Waltham

CELESTIAL ABODES OF ABSENT SOULS

Blood on my hands
Blood in the box
Fear in your eye
A tear in my eye
Life leaves you,
A passing friend.
Half eye,
Blessed closed eye
Life has quietly passed on by
Another star alights the sky
And I am left asking why?

The years pass slowly by as I gaze perpetually at night-time stars
and like Arabic bazaars, I am bewildered.
Is this where you are old companion?
Is your soulful essence there?
Do I have to invent a God to join you?
I will never be the same again
We have a sacred land together.

Rhys Wyndam Warren

FOREVER FRIENDS

Through childhood, teens and adult years we find our special friends
Some stay near and some go far
But a friend is always a friend
When you meet a friend after many years
A warm flicker in the heart
Fans bright so fast to bring you close
You feel you were never apart
It's good to remember friends old and new
A friend is a friend, always for you

True friends accept our failings, seeing our good points shine through
Friends are glad to support, to comfort and listen too
Trying to help when the road isn't clear
They may tell you things you'd rather not hear
Good friends can be really blunt with you
But you know deep down they are just being true
You trust the depth of a true friend's care
And you know for you they will be there

Friends are there for laughter and to share in your good times
And when you are really down they can see the signs
We all have many acquaintances adding variety and spice to each day
But a true friend is a treasure
A true friend is forever.

Maureen Stewart-Condron

REMEMBER LOVE

My bed is but a nest in trees
Shaken by a loving breeze,
Holding my beloved's hold
In each other we grow old

To honesty we search
Grasping to life's perch,
Tight as bind, she does grasp
We do both wish to clasp

Her flesh peached skin
We smile and grin,
Kiss thy summers spring
I do but want to sing

First as last
Months have past,
Still my thoughts of pleasure sought
I am but a pleasant thought.

J Sanderson

SPECIAL FRIENDS

As time passes by,
We all have friendships
That grow old and die
Our friendship is strong
It rises above troubled times
To let me re-gain peace of mind
It allows me to carry on
And nurture the will to survive
In both our hearts
We possess so many happy times
That remain only yours and mine
Nobody knows better than me
That friends come and go
Into the future I cannot see
But we will be friends forever
As long as there is hope left in my heart
We'll be together
And never part
I can always depend on you
So thanks for being there
Mum, I'll love you always
Even when I drive you to despair
I know that you'll always care

Lindsey Robinson

SOUL MATE

There is nothing like it,
Money can't buy it,
You can't see it, but you know it is there.
When happiness seems to have gone out of fashion.
Arms will enfold you, with care and compassion.
When the dark days are over,
And your tears are now dry,
Hope will return, like the incoming tide.
Remember these words, that have just passed my lips.
The best thing in life, is a loyal friendship.

Eileen Bolan

DAYS

On our walk where the hawk swoops low,
I feel a peace that only we know,
The skies are full and awaiting change,
The leaves are damp and littered with paws.
I want to tell you,
That you are my amity,
The pull on my cord,
The weight to my string.
We smile in the wind,
With cheeks glow and bright,
Heading for commonplace against our will,
Yet I do not dwindle,
I have calm in my mind.
The aroma, now polished,
Is with me to stay.
The memory of engagement is mine to recall,
Until we connect once more.

Zoe Young

FRIEND - SISTER - MOTHER

You're there, you're always there for me
And there can be anywhere, at any time of the day or night
Yes, you're always there for me.

You give me back my courage, which I sometimes lose
And help me to see clearly through the fogginess
Through the dismal disarray of my thoughts
Your strength flows into my veins when I am weak
Urging me to fight through helplessness and abandonment
Which sometimes comes now and then to engulf me

You are my sister, my mother
The conductor who quietens the noise inside me
Settling each piece back in its place, ready to begin again
In harmony, in order, able to try one more time
Yes, you are there, you are always there

To laugh with me, through golden precious moments
When life is heaven, when everything is more than beautiful
And life is too intoxicatingly good
When together we walk on the path of reality, down to earth
And share each others deepest thoughts
Talking for hours and hours, respecting each other
For the value which each of our lives give to one another

You are always there, to see my cry
Crying tears of happiness and love
And with me, you cry too, we both cry, for each other
Because we are always there for one another, always

I am so lucky to have you to be a part of my life
And for me to be a part of yours
For in the short space of a life time
I have been touched with the wealth, a true wealth
Of a friend

Odette Timmons

TO MY FRIEND MISS CLARK

Miss Clark was always there
A friend indeed without compare
Her heart remained young
Always ready to join in the fun
With Darren my son.

Around the fire they played
She sat on a little stool
She and Geoffrey had made
With sticks and matches she saved
There was soon a pretty blaze.

She lived her life as a Christian should
Offering to help how best she could
Her garden was a bit of a maze
And on it a friend's pony and donkey grazed
A bush of holly was made into sprays
Given for gifts and church displays
In spring at my door some snowdrops would lay
God bless Miss Clark
See you again some day,

Yvonne Harding

I THINK OF YOU OFTEN

I think of you often my absent friend,
although you are not here,
We started school together,
Friends for life it would appear.

We grew up through our ups and downs,
Both started courting young,
Left school, got married, had children,
Life just seemed to go on.

But everything changed my absent friend,
When cancer took a hold,
You left this earth aged 36,
Together we won't grow old.

I think of you often my absent friend,
And when I'm feeling down,
I think of your happy carefree ways,
And wish you were around.

I miss you - my absent friend.

Jayne Smith

DESTINY

I stand and look at you -
And I find myself staring
Into the depths of both our souls
The strangest feeling stirs
Deep inside of me -
I see myself looking into
The face of destiny.
I look at you,
And calmly know.
That there is nowhere else
That I need to go.
Nobody else could be me feel,
The heart binding glory
When you look at me.
I love you always -
Please always be.
That which we are together -
Each others destiny

Vanessa Lloyd Williams

POEM ONE

It doesn't matter where we go
Whatever plans we lay
If we will only let it be
New friends will come our way

It isn't just today we live
Tomorrow comes as well
The seeds we planted yesterday
Are sure to grow and swell.

Give a welcome approach as you pass by
With a cheery smile say 'Hello'
'Twas just at that time you were meant to be there
As she poured out her problems once more.

Whatever comes and whatever goes.
With friends close by our side
Our life enriches every day
Joy, love and peace abide.

Of course there's still our furry friends
From whom we learn no sin
Their wagging tails, their loving ways
Just pour affection in.

We've just one absent friend to meet
The friend of every friend
The friend who's with us all our life
Until our journey's end.

Elizabeth E Wallbank

FRIENDSHIP

Friendship is these two children,
    Sharing everything,
Bits of paper, coloured beads,
    Shiny stones and bits of string.

Friendship is *sleeping over*
    Staying up till very late,
Sharing gossip and secrets,
    Every detail of last night's date.

Friendship is when you have problems,
    And need to talk them through,
It's endless coffee and patience,
    It's having someone there for you.

Friendship is unconditional,
    Full of laughter, sometimes tears,
It sees you through times, bad and good,
    It strengthens with the years.

Friendship is brilliant memories,
    Pictures of the past,
Lots of special times spent,
    Since the friendship mould was cast.

So if you find true friendship,
    Let it breathe and let it grow,
You'll find it's worth much more than gold,
    Believe me, I've found it, I know.

Brenda Barker

GRACE

Remember how we laughed
When we passed upon the stair
We'd dance away our heartaches
And sing away our cares

We'd run away at lunchtime
And trample through the grass
We'd smash their old chipped china
And wait for shifts to pass

At sixty you were older
I just seventeen
You taught me how to cook
And you taught me how to clean

Twenty years have passed now
There's been good times and some bad
And though we're often parted
I'm very seldom sad

In all the years I have known you
You've always been a friend
And even though you're eighty
That bond will never end.

Sheila Williams

REMEMBER

Remember - when we met 'twas wonderful,
Imprisoned lives became more colourful,
Two minds conjoined, no longer incomplete,
Freed spirits soared, challenges to meet,
Our new alliance was so powerful.

But then, a parting made us sorrowful,
So we pledged we would not be forgetful,
Determined that we would not face defeat,
Remember.

Though others tried to deem it fanciful,
Parting made our memories meaningful,
Our sensitivities were bittersweet,
Such amity is never indiscreet,
Soul-mates in harmony - 'twas beautiful,
Remember.

Drew Michaels

ORDER OF SERVICE

She walked down the aisle in her gladness
On the arm of her father, with pride
And the air in the church was electric
As her loved one awaited his bride
Her father, fulfilling his duty
Relinquished his charge to be wed
Touched by the grace and the beauty
Of the child that his marriage had bred

She walked down the aisle in her sadness
Supported by mourners, distressed
And the air in the chapel was muted
As her loved one awaited his rest
His widow, fulfilling her duty
Relinquished the man she had wed
Serene, sustained and supported
By the strength their marriage had bred

Wordsmith

KATY

Her short blonde hair
And light blue eyes
Her moody touch
Her stroppy sighs

Sometimes we argue
But not for long
Most of the time
I'm in the wrong

We talk about our dreams
And our different fears
We've laughed and we've cried
And always share our tears.

All I want to
Make her see
Is how much her
Friendship means to me

I'd be lost without,
Her gentle touch
No-one has a friend
Like mine who means so much

All of six years
Has been worth everyday
My friend is the best
How much more can I say.

J Humby

SOUL MATES

You were such a tomboy, I was quiet and shy; we got on so well
    together - who knows the reason why?
Friendships somehow just happen, there's no explaining it -
    You and I we got it right - I'm so glad we did.

Gone days of hockey sticks and girlish tricks they long since
    passed us by, but the memory still lives with me of the
    twinkle in a dear friend's eye;
Nothing seemed commonplace in the company of you - the colours
    were much brighter, my spirits felt much lighter, the sky
    a brilliant blue.

Ours was not a smooth-run course, school days weren't much fun
    Although there was a cheerful side with days of simple
    pleasure - where should we go, what would we do -
    excitement without measure;
Walking through sunlit woods dreaming of our future - hand in
    hand 'twas a golden land - was there anything better?

We made the grade our plans were made our separate paths to
    wander - through all the years of joy and tears our
    friendship grew much stronger;
You told me all your secret hopes - your worries were my own;
    We neither fame nor fortune made but we were not alone;
You gave me such encouragement to follow through my dreams
    But in real life as well we knew nothing is all it seems.

Then fate stepped in and you are gone forever - to have been
    your friend to the very end a bond no-one can sever;
Wherever time may take me, whatever I may do, there's a space
    within my heart that belongs only to you;
My world has been the richer for having a friend so true.

Anne Goodale

FRIENDS ABROAD

Christmas cards sent to foreign places
Bring snaps to mind of friends' faces.
Do I just write once a year?
I want to keep in touch but fear
That my routine of daily life
Is boring.

Friends who live in Britain can
Be reached by 'phone at random and,
Depending on the mood, can be
As near as sitting on my settee.
But you, who are too far away,
Miss out.

Have your children grown so much?
They were babes when we last met up.
Are you going grey like me?
I still see you as you were - carefree.
But now - bowed down with family cares?
Keep laughing.

The secret is to write at will.
Turn off the telly and be still
Write at any time of things
That conversation normally brings
Alive. Have we forgotten how?
Let's try it.

Sally Newton

FRIENDSHIP
(Dedicated to my sister, Mary)

Friendship is the sweetest thing
Though absent, my sweet friend is
      and far away - in miles, that is.

Closeness is the strongest thing
Where bonds of *true love* exist
And stronger still, love doth grow
      for me and my dear sis.

Thanks be to God, for this
And for all the blessings friendship brings.
Friendship makes the heart to sing
Sets the spirit free, like a bird on the wing.
Higher, higher, still, we go
      now our ages total 120.

No telegram, have we received,
for our ripe friendship - from the Queen,
But overjoyed we are, to know
      that what we have, and share, suffices.

Our predilection is for 'friendship'
One that's stood the tests of time.
      I am hers and she is mine.

Praise be to God for this
      and for this most precious gift!

Jenny Gill

SPECIAL FRIENDS

Special friends are hard to find
They really are a treasure
And if you're really lucky
They can fill your life with pleasure
But sometimes they do silly things
Which cause you lots of pain
And you end up falling out
Then making up again
I fell out with Sharon
Told her to stay away
And now I have to live with it
Until my dying day
I can never say I'm sorry
For the hurtful things I said
There's no way I can make the peace
For I've been told she's dead
We did everything together
Danced and sang all night
Then we'd walk home arm in arm
We were a sorry sight
We were full of hopes and dreams
And shared our secret wishes
She would pour her heart out
While I did the dishes
She had a voice like Patsy Cline
Her singing was really great
and I would give up everything
To have her back as my mate
I know one day I'll join her
And things will be as before
Then perhaps she'll forgive me
And we'll be mates once more

Corinne Tuck

TOGETHER FOREVER

It started as a friendship
And became something much more,
Our friendship suddenly blossomed,
And love came through the door,
Each moment shared with you,
Brings warmth to my heart,
To know we're now a couple,
And that we'll never be apart.
You make me feel so happy.
Just knowing you are there,
I'm really glad to know,
We've got this love to share.
Each memory of you,
Is a thought encased within my mind,
Of times spent together,
That no-one else will find,
Our love will surely blossom,
As we stay together,
And just the same as our friendship,
It will last forever.

Kelly Hall (16)

BIG PETE - LAST ORDERS MATE

Tears will fall,
As seasons end.
The last call,
For you my friend.

Tears may never leave,
Like ghosts of a sort.
Hearts that grieve,
Will be forever sought.

John Arthur Gilman

FORTY YEARS ON

Friendships start in many ways
Ours goes back to childhood days
We shared our fears, and shared our fun
Not caring what would come.

Teenage years brought happy times,
Until the wind of change rang out its chimes,
Our times together wcrc, but few
But, friendship stayed for me and you.

The twenties came, and still more change,
Our lives began to re-arrange.
Boyfriends came, and then they left
Some, causing us to be upset.

Then, off you went to distant lands,
But still that friendship stands.
You found your man, and I found mine
Our lives became quite sublime.

Our letters - well, just once a year
Help to bring that friendly cheer.
The sharing of our lives continues,
Even though there's many wrinkles.

In forty years, no, maybe more
One visit's all we've scored.
But though our shores are far apart,
Friendship stays within the heart

Gwen Hare

FRIENDSHIP

A good friend is like perfection
    so very rare
Whenever you need them
    They're always there
You know they will never cease
    To care
They are like a leaning post
    When you can no longer stand
As you become shaky
    They hold your trembling hand
The friendship they give is vast
    Like our land.

Yvette Herbert

A FRIEND

A friend is a precious
And wonderful thing
Someone you can talk to,
Someone you can ring.

Someone you can call on
In times of trouble
And you know for sure, they
Will be there at the double

Not to chastise you, if
You are in the wrong.
But will soon make you smile
Before very long.

Someone to share your
Joys and your sorrows
Not just for today, but
All your tomorrows.

Pim Foster

LIFELONG FRIENDSHIPS

Many full moons have shone
As the decades move on
Etching fine lines on each face
In their hearts they all know
As these friendships just grow
Loyalty and trust take first place.
When fate does decree they seldom each see
And for days do not mention the name
With distance between, and a long time not seen
Still count them the best in life's game.
In times of despair the problem to share,
For support when in trouble is a blessing worth double
Knowing there's a friend to rely on,
They won't make a song to point out you're wrong,
And you wouldn't think twice to take some advice,
And there's always that shoulder to cry on.
Good times have been had, for which all were glad
Pleasure, fun and laughter together,
Each family with pride, standing beside
Applauding success in another.
But when comes the bad, and there is no job
None have to plead, they all know the need,
And willingly give a few bob.
As time takes its toll,
Whate'er may befall,
If trust, love and respect still remain
Through the years to the end,
Then that's a true friend,
With such values in life all must gain.

Beatrice May Roberts

PAST FRIEND

Hello dear friend
what has happened to thee,
You're a shadow of your former self
half the one you used to be.

I've often wondered
what has become of you,
We don't see you around town
like we used to do.

I've heard many tales
I've heard you're on drugs,
so I've not kept contact
as it's a game for mugs.

You say you're on medication
well that's a different story,
I see from your face
You've lost the power and glory.

You used to set the town
alight with your panache,
nowadays it appears to me
You're very short of cash.

I'm glad I met you today
but I see you struggle with living,
Your eyes lack their lustre
but your soul is ever giving.

Mental breakdowns take their toll
but recovery from drugs is the worst,
take your time to get better
but please put yourself first.

R H Elliott

FOUR YEARS ON

Where is he now?
He's deep within my mind;
    My friend, I think of him, I think like him;
    Precious memories stirred, flit in, flit out.
Where is he now?
He's in my private tears, never forced but forever -
    A glimpse of the past in a song, in a book,
    His favourite orange rose, a quiet robin on the lawn,
    Brief momentoes of his joys
    Now bring his joys to me - and are gone;
    I move on. I'm comfortable with that now.
Where is he now?
He's in the mirror, looking back at me
    In the guise of my own face,
    His features given with unquestioning love at my birth.
    He's in my own reflection and yet forever at my shoulder.
Where is he now?
He's resting high in the stars,
    The brightest and best and the first that I see;
    That's him, dark eyes twinkling,
    Reassuring me, saying 'night love'
    Like he always did. I close the curtains comforted.
Dad, where are you now?
When you were here I had no reason to miss you.
    We could come and we could go.
    It was safe to forget you.
    But now your cruel and lingering absence
    Keeps you here with me forever on my journey.
Where is he now and always?
In death he's in my life. He's in my heart. He's in my soul.

Michelle Taylor

A LONG DAY

It's been a long day, to make the night seem short.
The frost on the trees as crisp as your voice.
Make tea for myself and let it go cold.
Tidy your things, none of them old.
Those idle moments, well one or two.
There's the postman again - I thought it was you.

It's been a long week, I couldn't go out
With the wind and the rain, and you weren't about.
It's been very quiet though people did call.
Couldn't eat very much, now the grass is so tall.
Next week I'm away for just a day or two.
But I'll be home very soon, you know I hate to leave you.

It's been a long month but I get some fresh air.
I need some new clothes but I'm not sure I care.
There seems little point to visiting places
Or meeting new people and seeing old faces.
My eyes are now one, just my own point of view.
I don't want to be if I can't be with you.

It's been a long year, there have been ups and downs.
I looked at new homes without familiar sounds.
But the long nights are here and my memories fade
Of the few smiles that came and what progress was made.
I dread the cold days and that I might grow weary.
Are they so dark? Or is it fear within me?

Because it's been a long day and a long year before
But the day I lost you was the longest of all.

D R Wareing

SORRELLA

Sometimes thoughts of you come into my head
Of things you've done for me and said
I smile
That no meaning of the future, present and past
Our friendship was built with a foundation to last
I laugh
Of memories of experiences we have shared
You sat and listened, you really cared.
I wonder.
What you are doing and feeling
Your words of wisdom and healing
I remember
You comforting me when I was feeling down
Making me laugh by acting the clown
I realise
Times that we have had a row
It strengthen the bind we have now
I know
Although we are now so far apart
You'll always hold a place in my heart

Gill Moreland

ACROSS THE ROOM

I used to see you across the room,
You were always smiling and laughing
Talking with friends,
But you were always happy.
Now you have gone.
The room is silent.
You are no longer there smiling and laughing.
Your friends are all silent,
But your presence is still here.
Your memory forever lives on.

Rachel Cole

FRIENDS

A friend's the one who's always there,
Tells you that they love and care
Your secrets keep and never blab
Perk you up when you are sad,
Put you straight if something's bad.
Tells you you're completely mad.

They'll share a lunch, enjoy a chat,
Compliment you on your hat.
Lend a pound when you are broke
Fill your thoughts with joy and hope
Help out when you cannot cope
Never treat you like a dope.

You miss them when they're far away
Look forward to returning day
Without our friends where would we be?
No-one to share a cup of tea
If there weren't friends for you and me.

Barbara Shaw

TRUE FRIENDSHIP

How would it feel to have a friend that would die for you
And give up everything in the world, if you asked her to
How would it feel if she moved away, yet came to your aid at the
                                                                              drop of a hat
And gave you her last penny if you needed it, and things like that
I'll tell you, it would feel absolutely great to know you have a friend to share
All your problems, and know that she's always there
I have such a friend, I have for the last 22 years
And she's comforted me in many times of tears
She's never let me down, she's always helped me out
That's what True Friendship is all about.

Amanda-Marie Foster

ALWAYS THERE

When you fall
Friends are those
      who lift you up,
      dust you down
mirror for you
      who you are
Pour balming oils
of love and reassurance
on tangled wound-up
      mind coils
watch each loose and bounce
uncurl, release
balance to wholeness of you
Then stand back
      in silent support
watching affirmation
as with renewed strength
      and vision
you set out again
On your own path
      In your own direction

Karen Bayly

JUST A FRIEND

A lover, a friend no more to share
Can't come round no more will dare.
You see she found out once or twice
We spoke on the phone, she's really quite nice.
She told me things that you both had done.
She even told me you both had a son.

I just sat here and took the lot
So I added my bit about my new cot.
So you thought that you were happily wed.
When he left your house he got straight in my bed.
It wasn't long after a baby we'd have
In seven months time to feed, change and bath.
'I don't believe it, it's all just a lie'
'I won't believe it, I'd rather just die'.
'I won't let him see her I know it's quite sad.
'For a little girl growing up with no dad.'
It all turned out very well in the end.
He does see his daughter I still have a friend

Jackie Drabble

MY BEST FRIEND

All my life I've searched to find
A friend so close they'd read my mind
To love, to laugh - there's nothing to hide
In you my friend I can confide
All my secrets with you I share
My inner soul with you I bare
It seems to me I've known you forever
Cannot imagine not being together
And even though we're far apart
You know that you are in my heart
I couldn't ever say goodbye.
Without you now I know I'd die
There's only you - there is no other
You're my soulmate, friend and lover
Therefore, to you I give my life
Can't wait, my love to be your wife.

Jacqueline M Arkell

DISTANCE NO OBJECT

A party invite.
Ten long-distance birthday cards.
Friends reunited.

Your Indian skirt
with cart-wheel legs underneath.
That familiar sway.

Conversation wine,
each mouthful held, kept, savoured,
held in warm, cupped hands.

Vintage photographs
rose coloured by memory
seen through new glasses.

Your nurturing gift.
Appropriate. So like you.
Our picture, hand framed.

Permanent and fast,
so instant like superglue,
was our special bond.

Time has not diffused
your keen eye and that rye smile.
We will meet again!

Chrissy Smith

ODD LETTERS

Hi Val, I know that it's my turn to write -
I think I might have enough time tonight:
As I hear girls' laughter from up the stairs
I long for our days on those hard school chairs
Where we sat side by side - giggle, giggle,
You did our sums, to me such a riddle:
Sir's little angels, we could do no wrong,
To *Music Time* programmes we'd sing along.

Then we were parted by that IQ test -
As partners our work had always been best.
From then on, at school, we were on our own,
Our friendship continued, thanks to the 'phone.
We'd take our kid brothers over the park,
Enjoy a good grumble, or have a lark.
That's until boys took you out of my life,
And one of them even made you his wife.

Thirty years later, what makes us still write?
Why do my thoughts turn to you, Val tonight?
Is it because we have both got two girls,
Or maybe our childhood hate for our curls?
We can't tell the reason, but I am sure
If we lived closer I'd knock on your door.
Our friendship is such that we can depend
On getting odd letters right to the end.

Jackie Silverwood

FRIENDS

I have had many friends throughout the years
At school there were always some to share tears
Of growing up in a rule filled land
Of do's and don'ts shattering devious plans

Friends who came to parties, friends who stayed
Old friends who vowed they would remain
As loyal as a puppy till death do we part
They were the friends that broke my heart

As years have passed so friends have strayed
Christmas cards dwindle, their memories decay
New friends are born and found some way
My best friend now I see each day

He is the lasting friend that I know
He's right behind me, wherever I go
He's there at the end of the day till dawn
With me all night and every morn.

He's the one I can talk to relay my fears
He'll give advice and wipe away my tears
He's the man I married long ago
My childhood sweetheart, the best I have known

Harriet J Kent

BOBBY

Battered, bruised and still used
By my love
Held warm in the crook of my arm

Threads bared, souls shared
In a nighty
That once matched my own

Thin on top from a crew cut he got
From my brother
Who said it would grow

My silent confidant
My secret knight gallant
We don't have to say
We just know

S Curling

GRANDSON

I saw him
He seemed to be
An embodiment
Of pictured bliss

Flash, flash, flash
We took his picture
Till it hurt

We knew of course
That when he went
With them abroad
Our huge delight
Was frosted, frozen

Kept like ice cream
Till the new delight
Unwrapped itself
At our next meeting

And with wafered pride
We covered him with kisses

Jack Segal

MY SPECIAL FRIEND

My special friend,
Where would I be,
Without your love,
Or loyalty?

Other friends,
Have come and gone,
They just don't share,
Our special bond,

A bond that stands,
The test of time,
Maturing like,
A vintage wine,

When times are good,
You share them too,
When times are bad,
You see me through,

We've laughed our laughs,
And shed our tears,
Expressed our hopes,
And voiced our fears,

You're always here,
In my heart,
Whether close at hand,
Or far apart,

Because you'll be there,
Until the end,
I want to thank you,
You're my *special* friend.

Michelle Henderson

THE WINDOW

The tall mysterious tree stood erect
Framed by the window
Each branch reaching for the sky
A blanket of cotton wool drifted across
Misty by nature
Misty by day
The embankment green and moist
Peeking behind curtains
Soul searching
Paths of adventure bisect fields of emptiness
Blinded by beautiful thoughts
Imagination turned to reality
Transparent failures amongst hidden achievements
A famine of society in a backward world
Found, yet forgotten
Every window tells a story

Janet Forrest

FRIENDSHIP

A friendship needs some caring to survive,
Mutual kindly acts to keep alive,
The warming flow of thoughts to one another,
Suspicion, doubt, indifference, to smother.
And if our paths divide go different ways,
Some contact must be kept for future days,
For when the glow neglected fails to burn,
Our friendship cools, and gives us deep concern.
Have we then reached a point of no return,
And lost the loving bond for which we yearn.

May Harrison

LITTLE JOE

Always faithful, ever true, courteous in manner,
Sometimes in sorrow, sad at heart, yet none would ever know it.
Little Joe they all called him, from whence he came,
Of parentage, it was a guess of many but for a fleeting moment.
Yesterday the cortege passed, as usual by the Mercat cross,
And heads were bowed in silent grief, while memories came
Flooding in of a waif found down by the Harbour.
Out at sea a ship passed by, the last one of the season
And one was left who cried and cried until they thought
He would lose his reason. Granny Win she took him in,
It was many years ago. He's no good to you,
Won't ever grow, some said with ugliness and spite.
Granny Win just shook her head and said a silent prayer.
Later on when schooldays came, they got an awful fright,
When it was found, Joe held his own, on Granny's
Leek and potato pie, always right.
Strong he grew, in stature slight, and Granny's
Smile to see him so, it was a lovely sight.
The rainbow was not in it
The scoffers stopped, and praise was heard,
So often in the town, of Little Joe,
And granny's favourite son.
Both are now in heaven, united in the sky
And tears of sorrow have been wiped,
Away from many an eye.
Farewell Joe our friend and guide
Far away you will now bide.

Marguerite Auton

ODE TO DIANA

Bright yellow Oxford Bags.
Deep red auburn hair.
I was fourteen you were sixteen.
Do you remember? Do you care?

We shared so much laughter.
We dried each others tears.
Our friendship outlasted all the men,
As we marched through twenty years.

We planned our golden years together.
Until *he* burst into your life.
Suddenly you had left me alone.
When you became *his* wife.

I raise my glass to Auld Lang Syne.
Memories race through my head.
A tear trickles down my face.
Is our friendship really dead?

Diana do you ever stop and think?
Do you feel the loss so deep?
Have all your memories really gone?
Or do you make them sleep?

I have enough memories for two.
I won't lose the ember.
My memories will last forever.
When I sit and I remember.

I raise a toast to absent friends.
I look forward into future years.
I know we will share lots more laughter.
We are destined to dry each others tears.

Jane Webster

FOREVER FRIENDS

You were my friend
You still are
Where are you now
I want to know
I hear your voice
Your laughter too
Such a pretty face smiling at me
Where are you now
You listened to me moan
You saw me cry
You comforted me
and took my hand
Where are you now
I need to know.
There's more to say
But you are not here
How could you go without saying
Goodbye
I need to know
I know you can hear
You're still my friend - this
I know, I know.

M Warne

TED'S REWARD

Here am I all alone
Looking ragged, looking worn.
My legs are floppy and wearing thin
My body losing padding within.
Eyes, I've only one left now
Nose hanging on by a thread somehow.
Arms are weary and getting weak
My head still nodding, not even a squeak.

Time has really taken its toll
Another for the dustbin, oh! No!
Many happy hours of cuddles galore
I bet you couldn't beat my score.
Always happy with a silly little grin
Giving love and affection to all within.
I'm proud and honoured to have been a good friend
Reward! Going on display until my journey's end.

D Barrett

CLAIRE

You've always been there for me
A friend through the years;
Always sharing the laughter
And drying my tears.

Our first days of school
We shared arm in arm.
In the midst of the unknown,
You kept me calm.

We wrote when I moved
And our letters got longer.
We might have lost contact
But our friendship grew stronger.

Our childhood days are over,
We work instead of play.
The serious tones of adult life
Now echo through each day.

Our lives have taken different paths
But on this I can depend;
No matter what the future holds,
You'll always be my friend.

Fiona J Saunders

A FRIEND IS NOT JUST FOR CHRISTMAS

They were both born in 1931 when recession was at its height
And both working and middle class families found balancing the budget tight.
There was little gainful employment and money was very scarce
But families made the best of it - it could hardly get much worse!

Though their backgrounds differed, somewhat, firm school friends
                                                    they became
But, in truth, their early interests could hardly be classed the same.
Mary was bred in the country and enjoyed being an only child
while Stella was the middle daughter of three, yet always meek and mild.

The reason they came together is not hard to understand
As Mary sought companionship and Stella needed a helping hand.
They became almost inseparable throughout their whole schooldays
And, not surprisingly, friendship remained during their early working phase.

They both joined the local tennis club and turned up with all the gear.
Casual boy friends came and went as each pursued her chosen career.
But, in their middle twenties they both went their separate ways
Keeping contact by correspondence, especially Christmas and birthdays.

Mary married but Stella stayed single, as she still is to this day,
But the friendship fostered sixty years ago has still not withered away.
Testimony to this is revealed, even when they are far apart,
As the telephone keeps them up-to-date with many a *heart to heart*.

As the latter years passed by, friendship bound them more together
But, like all secure friendships, it blossomed regardless of the weather.
Fair weather friends may be numerous but those, in hard times, who
                                                    answer the call
Are the only true friends throughout one's life and are the best
                                                    friends of all.

John W Skepper

OLD AND NEW

For twenty three years
    You've been my friend,
Could this be the beginning
    Of the end?
Our minds have always been as one
We're still together
    (Though you're gone)

We shared the laughter
    and the tears,
Together rolling back the years
Now you're on a higher plain
Just waiting 'til we meet again

As we both rang in the new year
We never guessed the end was near,,
I even dreamed of you that night,
As usual, you said 'It's alright.'

Just before God set you free
You tried to draw some strength from me.
Our friendship has not gone away
I feel your presence everyday.

They say that time does not stand still,
But I know that one day it will
We'll be together Jack, you and I,
At that grand reunion in the sky!

Barbara Fenner

THE RIVER

The walls of the old building
Are crumbling now to dust
And decay, as if just through us
Was it willed into existing.

Where are you now
I am thinking -
Between beginning and end.
Looking into another's eyes?
Seeing there the one I never kenned,

And where, success or failure
Is all the same. One leaf
In a book, turned;
A river crossed,
Never to return.

R Faulder

ABSENT FRIENDS

Inseparable friends, separated
To them it feels the world has ended,
loneliness, sadness, great distance combine,
An everlasting friendship, destroyed,
letter writing is by no means the same.

Once a shoulder to cry on,
another person to blame,
Now this relationship has ended, and cannot be replaced
the good times have gone,
memories linger, like her absent face.

While it was there, it was not appreciated,
now gone, our everlasting friendship has faded.

Emma Smyth

FRIENDS

Life is happier for the
friends we have made;
The things in common
we share;
We want time to go on
not for ourselves;
But for all the people
who care;
It's the doing and giving
for anyone else;
That life and happiness
depend;
The contentment of
life is easily summer up;
By the having and keeping
of friends.

Paula New

FRIENDS

My most faithful friends live in the bathroom cabinet
Mister Max Factor and Miss Estee Lauder
Head turning accoutrements
Essential requirements of Miss Plain Jane
Disguises of Cleopatran proportions
Shaders, shadows, powders, potions
Faces of flattery ingeniously applied
Flaws vanished, eyebrows plucked, scents atomized
Reparation to complexion
Mask of confidence, visage of deceit
Duplicity hidden
Transformation complete

L Thwaites

MY BEST FRIEND

I've known her for a long time,
As long as I can remember,
I see her every day
From January to December
She dresses me every morning
Washes me and combs my hair
Gets my breakfast ready
Moves back my chair
She gets my home cleaned
From floor up to the ceiling
Says it has to be done
No matter how I'm feeling.
She does all the shopping
Pays the bills too
Makes all my decisions
Organises everything I do
My hubby says she's marvellous,
I must say I agree
Although I have lots of friends
My best friend is *me!*

Daisy May

FRIENDSHIP

I can still remember
The moment that we met,
A casual smile, a fleeting glance
Seemed nothing then, but yet.

It was the new beginning
Of something strong and true,
The very life blood of our souls,
Transferred between the two.

Quite gradually it happened,
And you became so dear,
You warmed my heart with strength and love,
Whenever you were near.

The years passed by,
But nothing changed
Together till the end,
Forever loyal you've always been,
My trusted, faithful, friend.

Anne Frances Wilson

FOND FRIENDS

We are atoms that float
down the river of life,
on our way to the
wide wide sea,
and life with its swiftness
its cares and its tears
brings its changes to you
and to me,
and if as the fast footed
years hurry by,
we lose sight of each other
at last,
let us always remember
that we, you and I,
were once fond friends
in the far distant past

Joan Wallington

RECALLED TO MIND

When we remember friends gone by
The price of electricity and food
What was last years news?
When Jimmy fell over the cat
Did he just get up and rub himself down
No, he sat, head in hands and cried

When we remember friends gone by
Like holidays and places
Or, Samantha, the one with airs and graces
She married a man, who beat her
No, she never gave up, she tried

When we remember friends gone by
The loves of our life
That gorgeous blonde called Olivia
Empty headed, she was not
She collected rich husbands and trivia

When we remember friends gone by
Memories, happy, sad, called to mind
Its nice to know that Jimmy, Sam, Olivia, John
Still make all my parties
No matter what day there on.

K Hemmings

ROPE LADDER

I climb
Old friend and mentor
Still I climb
Up life's ladder
Time
As forty Christmas cards
    do show
Friendship's acorns to
    stout oaks grow
In cursive messages
    lately written slow
To still remembered
    Callow growth on tip-toe
Stretching for life's swaying
    rope
Hope
You braced against each
    artful turn
Your distant grip
remaining firm
I cling
Old friend
I cling to life's ladder
Alas! Your Christmas cards now
Make me sadder.

John P Green

UNTITLED

Although you are no longer here
I raise my glass
With a smile and a cheer
Friendships are precious things
Like little birds with tiny wings
Looking back to all our yesterdays
Infant School - nativity plays
Brownies, Guides,
Brail your tent, make it secure
Campfire sing-songs
Who could ask for more
The thrill of our first double date
Shared experiences sitting on the old garden gate
Giggling till we were fit to bust
Crying till we were all cried out
Ready to rant, rave and shout
Period pains
Our first bra
Driving lessons
Our first car
Holidays, Christmas seeing the New Year in
Getting drunk
The first one with the wedding ring
Best friends forever and a day
Best friends forever
Then you went away
Leaving no letter not even a note
Only a large lump in my throat
Now you're no longer here
I still sit and shed a quiet tear
Friend forever friend that are true
I know now there will only ever
Be one of you

Mary O'Neill

MEMORIES OF OUR FRIENDSHIP

Do you remember a long time ago
Off to the shops we both would go
Pushing our prams it was great fun
Our motherhood had just begun

I'll never forget the little things
Going to the park and pushing the swings
The birthday parties trifle and cake
All the butties we had to make

Do you remember our weekly night out
Watching our numbers and hoping to shout
Our hearts beating fast and cheeks all aglow
We always looked forward to our night at Bingo

I'll never forget when my marriage did end
You really did stop me from going round the bend
I'll always remember the things that you did
Always at hand when I was flipping my lid

Do you remember when I was re-wed
That fateful day when my heart ruled my head
It didn't take long before things went wrong
But you were still there helping me to be strong

I'll never forget my nights of fear
At the end of my tether no more could I bear
You offered me shelter when no-one else cared
The comfort and warmth of your home you shared

Do you remember all of these things
Now I am wondering what my future brings
My only wish is that one day I'll see
A way to repay all that you've done for me.

I'll always remember
I'll never forget

Marjorie Coulthard

FOR ANDRÉE-ANNE

A gift
Shared,
A friendship no distance can annihilate.
Finding ourselves in each other.
We've found happiness
And a friendship which can survive any test.
Nothing can destroy these foundations of life
We have built.

Like Japanese flowers, petals open
We float downstream
On memories of golden days
When we'd dance away the dream.

Like an angel
You watch over me,
Opening my eyes,
Setting my mind free.

Our paths crossed
Our souls connected
Everything about life was perfected.

I'll never be able to express
How glad our friendship makes me,
Knowing we'll always be together
Wherever life takes me,
Spirits combined we will find
This companionship has no end,
You are a really true friend.

Nina-Ann Lewis

MY ABSENT FRIEND

We met at college in Ormskirk in our late teens.
You were from Paraguay, I from Derbyshire. Both were homesick.
Coping with college courses and learning independence
From parents and the practicalities of life was difficult.
We washed without a machine, shared an iron and board with others,
Shopped for groceries and invited groups of girls for supper.
We swam in the lovely warm water of the college baths,
Had scented shampoos in the showers and returned ravenous
For the 6.20pm meal. We sailed on a ferry across the Mersey.
As gulls followed in the furrows of the boat
They rent the air with raucous cries, never to be echoed
By the silent flightless Liver birds on the skyline.
We hitched a lift to Chester. I sat on your lap on the only passenger seat.
For fun you parted your knees and my weight fell to the floor.
From time to time we visited your grandparents in Wigan
And watched the black and white television.
You were an energetic partner for artificial respiration.
We became qualified first aiders. Upstairs on a double decker
We went to Southport via Scarisbrick and enjoyed films at the cinema.
Seats in the gallery at Liverpool's Playhouse cost us a shilling.
I edited 'The Crest' and you wrote about your childhood memories -
About the big South American cattle ranch, the cowboys in their sombreros,
About your parents and your brother, the dust of the February drought,
About going to school on horseback and being pelted by monkeys
In the forest: about the green parrots, jaguars and crocodiles.
After two years we received our invitations to the going down dance.
Jill and Julie played guitars and sang. With books and files packed
In our trunks, teaching certificates and appointments to schools expected
In the post, we said our goodbyes to student days and each other.
Our paths had parted but not for ever.

Vivienne Brocklehurst

FRIENDS

So who needs friends
    Not me

Some people are fair-weather friends
    While all's well they are there
But when the going gets tough
    That's when it all ends.

Some people are part-time friends
    Those you see at work all day
Or others in the evenings just for play
    These are our part-time friends

A real friend, now they are very special
    They are there no matter what
Good times, bad times, at work or play
    They stick by you come what may

Friends can be from long ago
    Or made yesterday on the bus
These friends will always be there
    A friendship that will grow and grow

These friends are true friends
    You can trust with your life
They are there from the start to the end
    These you know are real friends

Who needs these friends
    Me please

Josie Jessop

UNTITLED

The world can fall around us
with all life's ups and downs
never wanting freedom
from the friendship we have found.

We sometimes face the curse
of living and handling our tormented lives
through heavily weighted shoulders
only finding comfort, from a friendship that never dies.

With the security they offer
forever loyal, who is always there
helping you through life's disasters
they'll be there because they care.

And cherish your friendship
to each and every end
standing the test of time
keeping their distance, that's a true friend.

Never wanting payment
for all they have done for you
they only want your happiness
sincere in all they do.

When lovers and family
shake their impatient heads your way
find comfort in your loyal friend
who's there when you need them, come what may.

J C Darby

GIRL JEN

She'll run you an errand, she'll lend you a dress,
Lovely girl Jenny is one of the best
She's always happy, daytime or night
She is always smiling, beautiful and bright.
Burst into song, ooh what an earful!
Never seems down, remains ever so cheerful.
With dazzling bright colours, she chooses to wear,
Jenny getting lost is the last thing to care.
Whenever I am with her, laughs by the score
Laugh till my sides ache making them sore
I often call her leery, sometimes a lunatic
She doesn't seem to mind at all, takes a lot of stick.
I tell Jenny secrets, she'll never be a traitor
'Cos everything's forgotten two minutes later
Her idea of fun would be, something that's rather jolly
Like jumping from an aeroplane, hanging from a brolly.
Jenny's trademark seems to be her ever colourful bins
Her innocence makes her lovely, she has no wicked sins.
Behind her mask of comedy is someone brave and bold
She's also kind and gentle with a heart of gold
For all the tea in China I wouldn't swap that gal
The day I met Jenny, I met my best pal.

Heather Lee-Hooker

FRIENDSHIP

For friendship's sake
How sweet the words ring
Your hand in mine take
And solace to me bring

Travel by my side
Uplift me on my way
Make smooth the pathway rough
With love's golden ray

I cannot bring you riches
Nor precious jewels that shine
Just prayers for his own blessing
From this loving heart of mine

Travel where you will
Yet however far apart
Friendship's love lies still
Within this loving heart

Life's joys and cares we'll share
Then *more* and *less* they'll be
While *one* at least shall care
God gives us Heaven's key.

Dorothy Ventris

DEREK
(Written in 1990 after the sudden and untimely death of my partner Derek Ryding who died at the age of fifty-two years.)

We had so little time together
But my love for you will live forever
You did not know we were to part
To leave me with a broken heart

We had no chance to say goodbye
When you were called away - to fly
And leave this earthly life
With all its trouble and its strife

I wish that I could see your face
Or hold you in a fond embrace
We were so happy you and I
Derek why did you have to die?

They say that time will heal the pain
But in my heart you will remain
For no-one else could ever be
As loved and cherished as you were by me.

I know one day we'll meet again
Albeit on a different plain
Then we'll walk together hand in hand
In that beautiful eternal land.

Mavis Boothroyd

A FRIENDLY MATCH

I had to shoot you.
I had to kill you.
From my grave I peppered you with hate.
Day after day the wind carried messages between us,
First it was anger, then it was fear
From me to you and back to me.
I could smell you, but I couldn't see you.
Then we met.
Like scared rabbits we bobbed out of our warrens
Was I the fox or were you?
I held your hand. Bloodbrothers.
We never spoke.
But we ran together,
We cheered together,
We even laughed together.
I could see my death in your eyes
Did you see yours in mine?
Time stood still, killing stood still, the wind was still.
You were my friend.
But then they took the ball away
We moved the guns, the goal posts gone,
We had another game to play.
How could I kill my friend. Maybe I didn't.
I see your face every day
Do you see mine?
The games are different now.
The goals are harder.
The wind still delivers its hope
I smell it every day. I know you are there.
My friend.

Belinda Hastie

A DISTANT FRIENDSHIP

Kitty and I have been friends
for thirty five years and some days
we tell each other everything
yet we've never met face to face!

The reason will soon become clear
when I tell you that my friend Kitty
lives far away in the USA
while I live in Leicester city!

Our only communication
is by airmail letter or card
we try to save for a flight either way
but finding the money is hard.

However, we keep up to date
with news of events that affect us
and family secrets are passed back and forth
'cause no-one would ever suspect us!

Two lonely young mums when we started
seeking penfriends - our last resort
now the years have cemented the friendship
in a way we would never have thought.

Nowadays when she sends me a photo
I look at the grey hair and lines
and know that the years are taking their toll
maybe soon we will run out of time.

So I'm having a go at the Lotto
and if I should win it some day
I'll make a quick phone call to Kitty
then it's next stop the US of A!

Doris Paul-Clark

A LONG DISTANCE FRIENDSHIP

The door opened,
    Scared eyes peered round.
She stood in the doorway
    Looking at the ground.

Her first day
    At a new school.
She knew no-one.
    She was trying to keep her cool.

We became best friends
    And were in the same class every year.
We could talk about everything.
    To me she became very dear.

After six years of friendship
    I had to move away.
I had no choice.
    I couldn't stay.

We never lost contact.
    We still visit, phone and write.
When I visit relatives
    I visit her and stay the night.

Many miles separate us
    And keep us apart.
But we will always be together,
    Deep down in my heart.

Bridging the gap of distance
    Our friendship lies strong.
And for ever and always
    It shall remain long.

Holly Foat (15)

POEM TO MY FRIEND

Your mind dances alone
                in space.
My words try to breach spheres;
                to catch
Your vagrant wits on hold;
                force memory
Of dog-days in summers,
                when innocence
Primped and loved and cried in
                our childhood.

I aim remembrance lances
                at your mind;
Of hot sweet night dances,
                the wine's joys.
How in the dawn, we kissed
                the lovely boys;
And the light of long years
                with he and he.
I finger locks to free
                grey clouds.

For you the snow-line came,
                blanketing.
You left slowly, sleeping
                in warped time;
But here your starving mind
                smiles vacancies.
Loves, births and deaths all gone;
                no yesterday.
Yours the drained, distant way;
                the ache mine.

Irene Hanson

SIXTEEN

College - all the excitement.
Enrolment day.
I was naive.
They called my name - I responded.
Sank shyly into my chair.
Margaret came forward - bouncing her ringlets.
Who was this person?
'I'm a Catholic,' she said
I warmed to her, she was different.
College was a challenge.
So was Margaret.
We became friends.
Christmas, every year since has been a
Time of renewing our friendship.
Long letters pour back and forth.
Now, in retirement -
Margaret, in her superfluous world of Los Angeles,
Me, in my 'two up, two down' in England.
We've never missed a year.
Thank you Margaret for showing me your world.
Hope I have taught you something of mine,
And rekindled old memories.
May it continue.

Doreen Palmer

FRIENDSHIP? OR ARE THERE REALLY ANGELS?

Looking for friendship?
It seems to have its upside downs,
because when you really need it -
it often can't be found.
Like umbrellas on a rainy-windy day
always blowing inside-out.
'Play properly' I want to scream and shout
- but easy-going friends have often
easy-passed away.
Friendship can be the fleeting breath
between a dagger and a kiss
or maybe can combine them both
(you ghosts of Judas know of this!)

The flag-waving, ultimate test
of friendship - lies quietly in time and space.
Only after time may we understand it best.
After all the battles and the arguments
have been sorted out - each one in its place.
But friendship *itself* is a funny friend,
its purpose is not always clear.
Telling each other so many things,
some we'd prefer not to hear.

But *our* friendship is the illumination,
carved from ever-changing, timeless, passions.
Your fulfilled promises of my yesterday's dreams,
In the penny-bright uncertainty of my drunken fashions
cause the understanding that
Our friendship bears the brightest torch.

Jon Tuffnell

BEST FRIEND

Do you know who my best friend is?
He is someone who never argues, never shouts
And never forgets who I am
Do you know who he is?
He is strong and silent
With me all the time
Never leaves me
Loves me for who I am
Do you know who I mean?
I will tell you who he is

Jesus is my best friend.

Paul Thompson

UNTITLED

'It's just another hurdle,' she said
and she was right, my friend
of thirty years or more,
our husbands gone
children scattered, scarpered.
Now this latest one
as big as beechers
brace yourself
scratches galore
tasks instead of tears,
'What did you expect a grandstand
view,' she said.
My friend of thirty years or more
'Come on, get up of the hard cold floor.'

Olivia Hughes

THROWN TOGETHER

Thrown together by a war
with no regard for rich or poor,
your lovely home you let us share,
those shattered men with souls so bare.

That grand old house amongst the Downs,
where men sat still with dressing gowns
pulled tightly round to block out thought
of all those places where they fought.

For many years I cooked and cleaned,
your love and friendship to us seemed
to fill the rooms and heal the mind,
you wrote to those they left behind.

You were a friend to all who came,
giving them hope and making them sane,
others befriended and gave their homes too
but I know in my heart they were not like you.

We kept in touch as the years rolled on,
our thoughts we shared of times long gone.
But then I heard of your sad plight
and now I'm here to share your fight.

That same old house on the rolling Downs,
full of memories, full of sounds.
I know their thoughts are here with you
with the same love and friendship that pulled them through.

Valerie Duffy

ODE TO AN UNKNOWN FRIEND

Through summer nights and golden days
I yearned for you through misty haze.
My tears of loneliness did flow,
As such as you I longed to know.
My hours seemed wasted, filled with nought
But empty laughter, selfish thought.
Without your form beside me there,
I neither loved nor could I care.

And then came autumn, crisp and dry . . .
A glimpse of you, you held my eye.
I liked you, knew you were the one
To cheer my soul, bring back the sun.
It seemed but seconds after this
When, tentative, you aimed a kiss
At my bewildered face, as firm
You clutched my hand and raised the germ
Of care and bonding blooming yet.
The times we shared! Could you forget?
Through winter chill we clung as one . . .
Till one dull day you killed spring's sun.
Murder most foul! Villain beware!
My friend, still yet for you I care!

Carol Rivas

NIGHT

Behind the trees, the sun sinks low,
And bathed in glorious golden glow,
Nature now prepares for dark.
The fox and rabbit, crow and lark.

And then a startled bird takes flight,
All nature seems to feel its plight,
So still they stand, no sound they make,
They know they're lives could be at stake.

For one false move, or one wrong call,
Could be a creature's last downfall.
Then darkness falls within the wood,
The night owl calls and is understood.

Nocturnal creatures all around,
Answer his call with exciting sounds.
The world outside is fast asleep,
But in the wood night watch they keep.

Then slowly moving badgers,
Glide in the dark and feed.
Some snorts and grunting sounds I hear,
The largest takes the lead.

Then sunrise comes, the night is over.
Rabbits munching on the clover,
Deer retreat to woods to sleep,
Into their holts the badgers creep.

Pauline Avril Denham

ABSENT FRIEND

'Let's go to the pictures'
You used to come and say
That was in the good old days
Before you went away

You and I were best friends
Together through our teens
Our lives took separate paths, but still
We know what friendship means

We never did lose contact
We always kept in touch
Your letters were like magic
They used to say so much

They conjured up such images
Of your new life abroad
I savoured every sentence
I soaked up every word

I never will forget you
Though time goes by so fast
In my mind you're here with me
A feature of my past

An overdue reunion
I hope this year will bring
We'll chat into the small hours
Discussing everything

Recalling all the good times
Holding back a tear
Delighting in the company of
The friend I hold so dear.

Deanna Margaret Hassan

MUM

My strength and my weakness,
Through troubled tears and pain
She's always been there,
My Mum has,
And she'll be there again
To help pick up the pieces
And help to dry my tears
She's suffered more than I have
Through all my troubled years.

I want her to be proud of me
And never feel to blame
That perfect health evaded me
And illness often came.
'It's not your fault,' I want to say,
'It's nothing you did wrong.
It's something God saved up for me,
For when I came along.'

I want to see her smile,
I want to make her glad,
I want to show her I have grown
And she should not be sad
Because I've had my problems
For these I've overcome
With help from friends and family
And, most of all, my Mum.

Jennifer Maureen Young (Deceased)

WHEN THE LIGHT WENT OUT

I held him in my arms, and he wiped
the tears from his eyes.

As we talked about the places we had been
and the people we had met, the tears turned to
laughter and a smile beamed across his face,
his eyes lit up like a child with his first bar of
chocolate.

I found myself praying to God, thanking him
for this gift of friendship that had been through
so much.

And now this light is dimming and we must
part, but what we feel about each other will
never flicker out.

A B Stearns

IS IT FRIENDSHIP OR LOVE?

A friend is a friend,
To the bitter end,
One who understands,
One who cares,
One who listens to your daring dares!
But knows you inside out and upside down,
One who knows, you are acting the clown!
To sum it up and put it nice,
One who loves you whatever your plight!

Lena Frances

LONG TIME NOW

Long time now;
We've been friends
Since the early summer
Of our lives

We played and laughed
And learned and knew
Together we grew.

Long time now;
We've stayed friends
Through the bad times
And the good

We've shared with each other
All the fine things
Life can bring.

Long time now;
We're still friends
At winter's approach
We're yet warm

Through the fair wind
And the foul weather
We've kept close together.

Long time now
Since I've seen you;
But we write
All the time

And each word reminds me
Of the fun and the tears
Rolling down the years.

Christopher G James

AN ENIGMATIC VARIATION

If I have given you a gift
it is to have woven you
into my life
so that,
contrapuntally speaking,
we are complementary.

We live the shadow for the other
and conceive another way of life.

Our independence
combines momentarily
to provide a coherent texture,
and food for a week or a year.

Your reflection of my thoughts and pain
stops disintegration.
They are caught, moulded
and interpreted by love.

Maybe
the tapestry of your being
is touched and tended
instinctually,

as a mother soothes.

Jill Wheatley

CARING FRIENDS

The nothingness enveloped me
I was alone and friendless
In a strange emotionless world - at sea
Numb and painless.

The protection of this state appeared
To build a wall impenetrable
Which all at once was safe, but weird
And unfathomable.

How could I then break through this fence
To laugh again and live in full
Find joy in being, and a sense
Of Hope, that starry figure, who'll . . .

Bring recognition once again of worth?
And happiness and friends
Who understand my shock, and then unearth
The route to reality which ends . . .

The sadness, anger and regret.
At once I saw this was my way
And grasped the hands extended from the net,
They pulled and tugged me out - I lay.

Exhausted, happy now and free from grief
I understood the value of true friends
Who gave me back identity - relief
From the despair, uncertainty, which ends . . .

To bring acceptance, love, serenity.

Elaine Howard

HANDS ACROSS THE WATER

Another land produced a friend, and sent him oversea.
Whilst stationed here in England, he became a friend to me.
I found it hard to understand the slang expressions used
But though some words were quite obscene, he kept us all amused.
So close were we that when he left my whole world fell apart
I felt the total emptiness; felt like a broken heart.
My world at once was empty, a brother now had gone
Would I ever see again, the smiling face of Ron?
Although we said we'd keep in touch I didn't think we would
I thought I'd said my last goodbye, and seen him gone for good.
My fears were all forgotten, when through the post one day
Came a letter from America, inviting us to stay.
The weeks ahead seemed endless, we couldn't wait to go
To see the friends we missed so much, and go so well to know
The long flight over water filled my wife with dread
The thing that made it all worthwhile was waiting up ahead.
Just as we cleared the customs hall, not knowing where to go
A hand clamped hard my shoulder, a deep voice said 'Hello.'

We stood and hugged and laughed and cried as only true friends can
Now gone the fear of losing this brotherhood of man.
It's always been a puzzle and men have often asked
Why? When you're having fun with friends time passes by so fast.
Too quickly now the time came round when friends once more must part
Again, that aching feeling took place inside my heart.
This time though things were better, the parting I could take
Because I knew, though miles apart I'd never lose my mate.
We've seen each other many times and frequent letters send
And often I have raised a glass to drink to Ron, my friend.

Peter De Beer

WISHING, WANTING, LONGING

Do I love her more?
Of that I can be sure.
As the years pass by,
My heart bids me,
No longer cry.
A warmth I feel here,
And so pleased am I,
To have this friendship dear.

It is so nice to see my friend,
And have her near,
Just once or thrice a year.
Demanding nothing.
Wishing, wanting, longing
To give more.

Who knows, some sunny day,
When Life's games do change
To flow another way,
The flames within our hearts,
May burn brightly once more.

And then if we do but dare,
That closeness once again,
We might share.

Until that time
I am content to know,
We are truly bonded,
By some spiritual intent.
And this love I feel for her,
And cherish so,
From my heart it will never go.
This I know.

John S Lovesey

MY FRIEND

I owe my friend so very much.
My story's not easy to say.
You see, he gave me all he had;
With his life he had to pay.

My friend's first home was humble, poor,
His timely birth stirred up many.
Some were fearful of who he was
Even though he gave love to any.

He grew up discerning all man's ways,
Knew devotion, denial, tears.
He travelled, taught, he healed the sick.
Gave compassion, love, his years.

He was skilled with his hands, clever and true,
Never boastful, conceited or vain.
In all he did he used his heart.
Innocent, convicted, in pain.

He offered himself upon that cross
To die, it should have been me.
He rose from the grave to live again.
Wherever I am, he'll be.

He wanted me to have that chance
To go to heaven one day,
To have a life worth living Now,
To talk to him; to pray.

And so these verses are written down
To vouch for his love for me.
His promises have stood the test of time,
For eternity our friendship will be.

Angela M Harris

ALONE NO MORE

I feel cold and it's chilly and everything's white
Not a person or noise or a whisper in sight
I then see a light and it's not far away
'Come follow me,' I hear a voice say

I go through a tunnel with colours all bright
And then through a door that's showing a light
I come into a garden there's a beautiful smell
There's flowers and sunshine and a wishing well

By the trickle of water I see a familiar face
She turns and she smiles with ease and with grace
It's been so long since I have seen her lovely smile
Forever and a day but it's all now worthwhile

'You've been gone too long,' I hear myself speak
I thought I was strong but now I feel weak
She seemed younger and different, I could not think why
I felt older and conscious and a little bit shy

She held me and took me to a bench in the shade
She kissed me and suddenly her voice seemed to fade
She got up to go and I begged her to stay
'Take me with you,' I heard myself say

We went through a door that was left open ajar
'There's no going back now you've come this far,'
She slipped her hand through mine and I followed her through
I did not look back - from the past to the new

'You've had and stood the distance of time
and now you are here you are really all mine'
No looking back through my tears I see love
to be joined with my wife who's in Heaven above

Lannette Lusk

UNTITLED

Thank you for being there
when I was alone,
if not in person
at the end of the phone.

Thank you for caring
what happened to me,
your eyes saw clearly
what mine couldn't see.

Thank you for actions
which at first seemed unkind,
but which helped me to understand
what goes on in my mind.

Thank you for giving me
faith in myself,
that I am worth something
not left on the shelf.

Thank you for curbing
my impetuousness,
and calming my fears
of deep loneliness.

Thank you for my future
whatever it holds,
be it good times together
. . . or memories of gold.

Sue Millett

REMEMBERING THE TERRAIN

I watched you smiling happily
Tall in the appalling polluted grass
Smoke painted grey
Pale pallor of chimney nostrils snorting
A breathing English death
Amongst the singing hymns
Though not yet stifling the smile of spring
The best I know

Lips chin and nose all grinning
Pleasure wrested from the trauma
Of disturbing hours of trade and domestic polish
Knowledge drawn from learned lines of years
Steady as the seasons
Quartered for weather and promises

Then it was
In the salt sobbing seawater wet
Of detestable goodbye brine tears
Roared my tiger striped cries
Clawing the hoping hot in my belly past

Now with the clotting of throats and chins
Memory thins
To the narrow and happy cameo of you
Never wearing eyes to realise
In my every evening and morning barking echo
During those peak and valley
Exploring forests with you.

Bernard B Michael

MEMORIES OF BILL

We had some laughs when we made fun
Of things he'd said and things we'd done
Talked of places to which we'd been
Interesting things we'd seen

So many likes and some dislikes
When nattering about our motor bikes
Then recalling memories fond
Of how we used to go by Bond

Talked about mechanical things
Levers, wheels and different springs
Sometimes uttered a sort of prayer
When starting on a car repair

Painting at Cliffe between the showers
Discussing veg and pretty flowers
Neighbours passing, saying again
'We could do with some more rain!'

Staggering from the 'Golden Ball'
But never really drunk at all
Could only laugh but couldn't think
Because we'd had too much to drink!

The time when we just said that if
We left the town to live at Cliffe
We'd have to improve at dry-stone walling
Else folk would shout 'Your boundary's falling!'

Such memories I'll keep until my end
Goodbye to Bill - Goodbye old friend.

Frank Rimmington

MY FRIENDS FROM ACROSS THE SEA

I was barely a month the first time I flew
Across the big ocean to a home oh so new.
I have lived here now for a decade and more
Yet I remember my friends whom I met before.
I wasn't quite five as I stood out on the street
Still hoping and waiting for someone to meet.

It was a return to the land of my birth
I was so excited, it's the best place on earth.
All of a sudden from a distance away
I heard two young voices calling me, 'Come and play!'
I replied with a, 'Wait!' as I ran to the door
I went into the room and heard my gran snore.

They live on a street that is close to my gran
So I try to visit them whenever I can.
I don't see them much since I live far away
But as soon as I arrive I go out to play.
My mother complains as I jump out of the van
That I really came here to visit my gran.

Oh Michael and Brian are such special mates
We play through the summer on bicycles and skates.
When the weather is good we play on the street
Almost any old game we are happy to greet.
We may go to the park to play on the big swings
Or there we play baseball and other fun things.

When the summer is done I must return home
But in less than a year I will come back to roam.
I think of the summer whilst I am at school
I remember the days where we played in their pool.
Yet the year that has passed does not hinder our game
For when I return good friends we will remain.

Geoffrey Quint

ALL MY FRIENDS

All my friends I have you see
Give me pleasure, give me glee
When my birthday comes a round
And my feet firmly on the ground
Our 'coffee event' is in full swing
Oh what happiness that will bring
Arms open wide? A hug and kiss
This is truly truly bliss.

At eighty one years old you see
One is happy one is free
To love and laugh in a hundred ways
Happy till the end of our days
All of my friends are of long standing years
Bring me happiness or bring me tears
Of joy that I have such wonderful friends
Over the years that never ends

God bless all these friends God bless them I say
To the end of my days I shall always pray
To keep young and happy for all to see
They are my lifeblood and I pray on my knee
That God will look after them as he has me
Over my years of trouble and strife you may see
That *friends* are invaluable and I pray
For all my good friends at the end of the day

M A Tubb

FRIENDSHIP

Friends - are people who care enough to help you
And to share your problems and your crises.
Who help you when they can and even when they can't,
When you are at the end of your tether -
They give you more rope to help you cope,
But not to hang yourself with.

To help you cope with thoughts, events and pain,
That, at times, get too hard to sustain.
Friends are people to cry with, as well as to laugh with;
They are the people who make your eyes light up when you see them -
Who make your steps easier, your baggage lighter -
You hope you have the same effect on them.

When *they* need a helping hand out of the swamp of life -
That *you* will be there with an outstretched hand.
Friends not acquaintances - give the support you know you need
And sometimes, from them, you find just what you need.

Friendship, like love, is a two-way street; not a giver and a taker;
Two givers and two takers, a balance and equality of mind;
A sharing, a caring and a giving:
Friends don't ever make you feel small
Or that your problems aren't problems at all.

They are there for you, as and when you need them -
Just as you are there for them.
But, the best thing about friends is being able to laugh with them.

So - let people know you care, you can even share
Some of their feelings; - and even if
You can only smile -
The memory of a smile lasts for ever.

Alice Englefield

A LASTING FRIENDSHIP

To a lady who lives in a land over the sea,
Who is enjoying her life now her country is free,
A friendship formed a long time ago,
By a soldier who helped fight the foe,

It was strange in the place he be,
But the people were friendly he had to agree,
To ease the burden of his task,
They formed a friendship that was to last,

Even in their hardships they shared food and homes,
For they knew he was lonely, so kindness they had shown,
When the conflict was over and new friends he had to leave,
And for comrades in sweet earth he had to grieve,

But then to say goodbye and go back over the sea,
Back to his wife and children his own family,
But he never forgot their friendship, and to his sons he told,
Never forget what they gave to me *friendship* more precious than gold,

Off these people in a foreign land, whose tongue he did not speak,
Who took him into their homes and with kindness did greet,
So son and his family did write to his friends across the sea,
To thank them for the kindness, they gave in their lovely country,

This lady her family and friends in our thoughts every day,
So we hope in the future all to meet we pray,
To talk about old times and tell how they feel,
Now this lady she's got a place in our hearts and her name is *Cecile*.

M L Fletcher

ABSENT FRIENDS

We think of those whom we once knew,
When we were young and tender.
When reminiscing in the past,
We are happy to remember.

We lived together side by side,
Our friendship strong did grow.
And when they moved to distance far,
We missed each other so.

When coming home from a day at work,
A cup of tea was there.
It made us feel o so refreshed,
And thankful for her care.

We helped each other such a lot,
In good times and in bad.
The knowledge that we had a friend,
Made all of us feel glad.

Tis twenty years since last we met,
And enjoyed each other's company.
The years slipped back as we talked and laughed
In perfect harmony.

At Christmas time we send a card,
Just to keep in touch.
And prove that friendship through the years,
Still means to us as much.

And at this special time of year,
For absent friends we pray.
And hope that in the future time,
We'll meet again one day.

I E Covell

MY ABSENT FRIEND

You were the best friend I ever had,
Always there when things were bad.

When I felt sad you were there,
All my troubles you would share.

I didn't have to ask you twice,
You were near to give advice.

There to wipe away my tears,
And help me through all my fears.

In all the years I knew you,
You always were so good and true.

All my pain you took away,
And helped me face another day.

Now you have gone and I am left with pain,
For nothing can ever be the same.

So I sit here all alone,
With my grief I cry and mourn.

My absent friend I will remember you,
For you were one of the chosen few.

I will miss you more than I can say,
Now that you have gone away.

God keep you safe within his keeping
Until the time comes for our next meeting.

My absent friend.

Valerie E Brown

GENUINE FRIEND

Rattle rattle upon the gate,
Here he comes my best mate,
Knock, knock, knock upon the door,
Here comes he this once more.

'Glad to see you,' I said with a smile,
'Come on in, let's talk for a while.'

Sit yourself down,
I'll make a brew,
Two sugars for me,
Is it one for you?

Tell me your gossip,
My good friend,
I'll tell you mine,
It never ends.

It's time to go,
He said goodbye,
Really so soon,
Do stay, please try.

No I have to go,
But I'll see you soon,
He put his cup down,
And left the room.

Goodbyes were said,
As he shut the gate,
We'll have to go out!
Sort out a date!

It's the last time I saw him,
He passed over the next week,
But memories are forever,
Of which I will keep.

C M Ellard

PITY THE LIVING

My dear friends don't you weep for me
because I am departed;
I know the pain you're suffering,
I know you're broken hearted.

It wasn't me in that wooden box
they buried down so deep,
but just the shell that housed me,
so dear friends don't you weep.

If you knew the happiness
that's overwhelming me;
The powerful, overflowing joy,
the painless ecstasy;

The awe inspiring beauty
my eyes take in with ease;
The all-embracing, steadfast love,
That perfect, perfect peace.

No more pain can touch me now;
No more will I cry;
If this is death, then dear friends
I was surely glad to die.

So dry your eyes, don't grieve for me,
my life is just beginning.
Don't pity the dead, who are safe at last;
Instead, pity the living!

Janet Greenwood

AN ODE TO THE STONE TENTS (AND THE FRIENDS I SHARED WITH)

It was a lovely day in September
The winter sun did shine,
As we stepped among the cowpats,
On our way to Ymas Barn,
We also shared our breakfast lunch and tea
With a friendly herd of Jerseys
Among the cowpat sea,
We walked into Bakewell
The puddings sampled well
The ducks and the cricket,
The afternoon was swell
We made it back to Pilsley
In time to call at pub
Stone tents are a pleasure
Back to nature you'll will find,
To share your time with nature
Is good, for all mankind.

Pauline Barker

GOODBYE

To say hello is easy,
To say goodbye is hard.
Remembering the good times,
can leave your heart so scarred.
People come and people go,
life can be unfair,
but if it's hard to say goodbye,
at least you know you care.
Friendship is a treasured thing,
worth its weight in gold.
Something worth remembering,
as we're growing old.

H M Berry

MEMORIES

The lamps outside have been switched on
The old lamplighter, has now long gone
To the folk he was a welcome sight
As he bid everyone, a cheery goodnight
He went along, whistling a tune
Finding his way by the light of the moon
Down the old cobbled streets, the old man tramped
The place came aglow, as he lit up the lamps
The lads and lassies gave him a wave
As the old man went on his way
Oh! for the days of yesteryear
Gone forever not I fear
But memories will always stay
Of lost friends, in the good old days.

M Caulfield

ABSENT FRIENDS

Let's raise a glass to absent friends
and remember the happy years.
We lived and loved, and laughed together
sharing our troubles and fears.
Although no longer with us now
their memory remains
they walk beside us daily
down life's many winding lanes.
I remember them with gratitude
their helpful kindly ways
the good advice, so freely given
when faced with difficult days.
Yes my friends, I miss you
more than I can say
always in my daily thoughts
as I walk the long highway.

Mairearad Wilson

THE NEVER-MOULTING WING OF FRIENDSHIP

Oh, tell me, Friend, what are these ties which bind my very being
                                                close to yours?
What is this kindred spirit, human or divine, which links our hearts as one?
What is it makes us seem, each to the other, wide and free as open doors,
Yet leaves us, side by side, at peace together when all other souls have gone?

For I, from you, crave nothing; nor, I know, do you crave anything of me
Except that our companionship of all these many years should still remain.
No profit here in earthly things, and each to each unfettered is - and free:
Yet both know well that in our bond of friendship lies our best and
                                                truest gain.

Eye to eye, in this most complex world, we rarely take an equal view;
When one of us predicts a tranquil passage, the other fears an angry sea.
In questions large and questions small, vast chasms yawn, dividing
                                                me from you:
One day, you claim, all life will cease; yet I, convinced, Eternity can see!

But does this count? Do diff'rences between us now or anytime prevail?
Can any disagreements fracture that stout link which joins us soul to soul?
Not so! Confronted by our yoking, they to insignificance do pale;
And joy or sorrow, loss or gain finds friendship indestructible and whole.

So, Friend, as we walk side by side, accepting from this world each shock
                                                and blow,
That power which binds us heart to heart will ever prove the truest and
                                                the best,
And if, from heaven's all-gracious hand, a liberal gift of years should
                                                kindly flow,
Then, through their joy or pain, our deep and constant friendship still
                                                will stand the test.

Ivor Haythorne

UNDER THE HOUSE

Dear Annie,
I was rummaging last night down in the cellar
when I came across an old shoe box, and found a pile of letters.

Down amongst the damp and cold, the rusty barbecue,
the cricket bats, the paddling pool, were memories of you.
The little square pink envelopes with cartoon cats and dogs,
our twelve year old imaginings, some sketches, Guide camp logs.

All neatly tied with webbing tape, elastic bands and string,
reports of schooldays, diary notes, the songs we used to sing.
We used my dad as postman (he gave you lifts to school),
Oh look! There's David Cassidy, remember he was cool?

And then from university, your second date with Tony
who you thought rather stupid, not to mention blind and bony,
But shaving off his beard, (the letter after this),
you changed your mind, and ended up in joyful wedded bliss.

Our letters fewer, boy friends first, our work, our play, our weddings.
Postcards from France, the USA, I feel like I'm retreading
all those summers, endless time all interwoven here.
A picture of your pregnant body, writing of your fear
of motherhood, of pain, of loss; we'd never see each other
once I became a businesswoman, you became a mother.

And later, plainer envelopes, with clearer recent news.
Your second child, your move to York, your monetary blues.
A gap of months, some scribbled lines, a 40th birthday card.
With busy lives the phone is quick, to sit and write is hard.

For many minutes, hours I think, I relived all our years,
the writing blurred by damp and mould, or maybe it was tears.
Shaken from sentiment by shouts - the kids up in the hall -
I must close now, my motherly and wifely duties call.

I'm glad I found that old shoe box, its treasures of our past,
so write again please Annie, and make it pretty fast.

Gillian Wilde

MY FAITHFUL FRIEND

I once had a great friend
Whom I loved till the end
She was always faithful loyal and true
Whenever she was proud I was never blue
I could tell her my most hidden thoughts
As we went on our long walks
But she would never judge, she would just hear
And I loved her very dear
She meant the whole world to me
And this anyone could see
I will never forget the day we parted
I was well and truly broken hearted
Just to live from day to day
Seemed to hurt in every way
People just did not know
How I could feel so down and low
I was going around as if in fog
All because . . . she was my dog

Trish Chandler

WHAT IS A FRIEND?

A friend is someone who'll always help you.
A friend is someone you'll help too,
A friend is someone to talk with.
A friend is someone to whom you'll give.
A friend is someone in who you'll have pride,
A friends is someone who you'll guide.
A friend is someone who you'll respect
A friend is someone you'll never neglect.

J Hart

INFORMATION

We hope you have enjoyed reading this book - and that you will continue to enjoy it in the coming years.

If you like reading and writing poetry drop us a line, or give us a call, and we'll send you a free information pack.

Write to

> Poetry Now Information
> 1-2 Wainman Road
> Woodston
> Peterborough
> PE2 7BU